Crochet

Techniques & Projects

By the Editors of Sunset Books

Lane Publishing Co. • Menlo Park, California

Foreword

Crochet is a popular traditional craft that has grown far beyond being only a homey pastime. In the case of contemporary crochet, yesterday's relaxing avocation has become today's art form.

Aimed toward the beginning and intermediate crocheter, our book features a comprehensive introduction to the basics of crochet — or a refresher course for a rusty crocheter of any level. Complete instructions are given for a wide variety of tempting projects. Included as well are a selection of advanced stitches and a delightful picture gallery of unusual and imaginative crochet pieces.

For their help, time, and advice, special thanks go to Cozzie Anderson, Teri Braasch, Taide Carpenter, Susie Clark, Sue Colson, Karen Cummings, Dauth Knitting School and Yarn Shop of San Carlos, Angela Di Vecchio, Jerry Anne Di Vecchio, Nancy Ferch, Folklorico Yarns of Palo Alto, Peggy Gutzwiller, Vicki Klein, Fah Liong, Holly Lyman, Binny Mortenson, Karen Oravetz, Chris Payne, Pajaro Dunes, Mr. & Mrs. William T. Riley, Gladys Robinson, Jeannie Rondo, Pat Scheidegger, Mildred Schuyler, Sherrie Sullivan, Nancee Ventimiglia, Allyson Welke, and Wild'n Wooly of Palo Alto.

Supervising Editor: Elizabeth Hogan
Research and Text: Lynne B. Morrall

Design: Terrence Meagher

Illustrations: Nancy Lawton

Cover: Rainbow ripple afghan (page 60), designed by Lynne Morrall. Photographed by Glenn M. Christiansen.

Executive Editor, Sunset Books: David E. Clark

First Printing October, 1975

Contents

It's easy and fun to take a ball of yarn and transform it into a textural piece of crocheted fabric. Learning to handle the yarn is a bit awkward at first. But with a little practice, you'll soon make your sample swatch look regular and even, and your fingers will begin to fly over your work.

Introduction to Crochet--
just loops of yarn

Why do crocheters love to crochet? For many, the craft is a kind of therapy, with the movement of the hands becoming a smooth rhythm that not only transforms a ball of yarn into an object but also soothes the spirit and eases away tensions.

To artists, crochet is a creative and stimulating art, a medium for displaying their talents in a soft and often three-dimensional form. The photographic examples in the "Creative Crochet" chapter, pages 70 to 79, attest to the artistic heights which crochet has reached.

Becoming acquainted with crochet

Crochet is one of the most approachable crafts. It's simply the looping of a continuous strand of yarn to form a variety of stitches. All you need to accomplish this are a crochet hook and some yarn. The crochet hook serves as an instrument to manipulate the loops of yarn.

Whatever your reasons are for wanting to crochet — whether it's an urge to make that smashing bikini or simply an eagerness to learn the craft — your first step is to master the basic stitches and understand the general techniques (see pages 10-33). Practice until the size of your stitches and the tension are uniform and your work looks loose and relaxed.

Once you feel comfortable crocheting, you'll find it goes very quickly. Your sweater, afghan, or shawl will "grow" right before your eyes. Soon you'll find yourself crocheting faster and faster, as if you're trying to keep up with this "growing" creature.

One of the most exciting ways to watch a piece evolve is to follow a color chart, such as the one for the slippers on page 44. Compare each stitch you make with the chart and photograph to see that the right color is in the right place. Since you're making flowers and stripes, you'll always want to crochet "just one more row" to see the pattern take shape.

Putting the basics to use

With the basics behind you, turn to the projects chapter (pages 34-69) to plan your first piece. If you're a beginning crocheter, select something easy and quick to do, such as the placemats (page 56) or the potholders (page 57). Leave the cape (page 39) for the more experienced.

Reading through the instructions, you'll notice that they are written in abbreviated fashion. Consider this style a kind of shorthand, rather than the exotic foreign tongue it appears to be. After some practice, you'll be surprised to find that the abbreviations will be second nature to you.

Consider crochet instructions a kind of recipe. Look them over before you begin to get an idea of what to expect. Translate the instructions into your own terminology or rewrite them in your own shorthand, if that makes them clearer to you. But be careful, you're adding a place for possible error.

Beginning crocheters should always stop at commas and periods. Don't read ahead after you've begun to crochet — that will only confuse and overwhelm you. If you start with a simple project and work up to the more complicated, you shouldn't have any problems.

Beyond the basics

An endless number of advanced stitches — variations of the basic stitches — await the adventurous crocheter. Use an advanced stitch as a pattern stitch or as an accent to add freshness or a new dimension to your work.

When you feel ready to tackle one, turn to our section on Advanced Stitches, pages 70-79. Let the stitch itself inspire you or let the intriguing examples shown in the photographs set your imagination to work.

Relax and enjoy

Once you've mastered the art of crochet, you'll be an avid crocheter. You'll love its versatility, for crochet has gone beyond the doilies of granny's day to become a craft, a creative medium pleasing to those whose tastes range from conservative through middle-of-the-road to avant-garde. The variety of items you can make, the number of stitch variations you can use, and the range of yarns and colors you can incorporate into your piece are almost limitless.

You'll find that crochet doesn't demand your total concentration. It's a relaxing craft, one that allows you time to think, daydream, or talk to a friend while your hands work away. And because it takes just a few materials, crochet is very portable. It can travel with you on a long trip or curl up with you under a tree.

So while you're crocheting, you're having fun. But you're also making something to wear, hold, or look at — something that reflects *you*.

Textural yarns *in a wide color range and hooks of many shapes and sizes are the tools of crochet.*

Tools of the Craft--

hooks & yarn

Although some crafts might tempt you to invest in such major equipment as a loom, kiln and wheel, or centrifuge, basic crochet requires only two tools: a crochet hook and some yarn. From this modest beginning, you can create anything from a simple doily to a three-dimensional sculpture. Then, as your interest and expertise grow, you may want to collect some of the miscellaneous supplies listed and pictured at the end of this chapter.

Hooks

Crochet hooks come in a variety of materials and sizes, but basically they're all the same shape. Each has a shaft, or shank, that determines the size of each stitch and a hook at the end to catch the yarn.

Metal and plastic hooks have a flattened area on the shank that serves as a grip for your fingers. The very large plastic and wooden hooks don't have this indentation because their shafts are large enough to be held comfortably. Afghan hooks have a metal cap on the end of the hook (similar to the cap on the end of a knitting needle) to hold the stitches on.

You can buy crochet hooks either individually or in kits at department, variety, fabric, and yarn stores. The kits are especially handy to have, for they contain in a box or case a good selection of hook sizes—chances are you'll have on hand the right size hook whenever you get the urge to begin immediately a new crochet project.

Types of hooks

Your crochet hooks can be made of steel, aluminum, plastic, or wood.

Steel hooks come very small and are used for fine work, such as doilies and lace.

Aluminum hooks are the most popular. Strong, smooth, and lightweight, they come in the most commonly used sizes. Almost every project in this book can be crocheted with an aluminum hook.

When possible, avoid using *plastic* hooks. They are brittle, and the hook is not as smooth and uniform as a metal one. However, you can use the jumbo-size plastic hooks with soft rope or very heavy yarn.

Until recently, *wooden* hooks have been available only in very large sizes. Now, small wooden hooks with intricately turned shafts are being carved by woodworkers in rosewood, walnut, and other hardwoods. Though these wooden hooks are beautiful, they're not as strong as aluminum and steel hooks and can snap under pressure.

Hook sizes

You'll find crochet hooks in a wide range of sizes, from a tiny, size 14 steel hook, to a jumbo, size K aluminum hook. (See the illustration below for a comparison of hook sizes.) Handcrafted hooks generally are not marked with a size but fit into the range of sizes of aluminum hooks.

Generally, the hook size you need will depend on the kind of yarn you use. For the most part, small hooks are used for thin yarns, large hooks for thick,

heavy yarns. This rule of thumb is most likely to be broken when you're crocheting to achieve a special effect, such as the loose, loopy stitch shown at left in photo on page 9. This stitch was made with a size K hook and fingering yarn.

On the other hand, if you use a large hook with a heavy yarn, the result will be a conventional, even stitch (see swatch at right in photo, page 9).

The tightness — or looseness — with which you crochet will also affect your gauge and can therefore influence your choice of hook size. (See discussion of gauge, page 29.)

Yarn

Renewed enthusiasm for such handcrafts as weaving, spinning, and vegetable dyeing has resulted in the widespread popularity of unusual yarns. Even conventional yarn shops now carry a selection of imported as well as domestic yarns. Irish tweeds and fisherman yarns, Mexican, South American, Scandinavian, and Greek hand spuns appear in shops, along with American yarns of traditional weights and textures and novelty yarns that duplicate the unpredictable texture of the imported hand spuns.

Weaving supply stores and yarn distributors are the best sources for the unusual yarns. Many of these businesses have mail order services that will send you yarn samples and a catalog of their supplies for a small fee. Look under "Weaving—Loom" and "Yarn—Retail" in the Yellow Pages and check craft magazines for advertisements of other suppliers.

When working with yarns of unusual thickness or uneven texture, be careful that your gauge (the number of stitches and rows per inch) is exactly the same as the gauge in the pattern you're following. If the gauge is off, the size of the completed project will also be off (see gauge, page 29). Always make a test swatch before you begin to crochet your piece.

Selecting yarn

Any yarn, twine, string, or rope can be used for crochet. Each is packaged and sold in its own way: macramé twine is sold by the pound or by the yard, leather lacing by the yard or in strips, hand spun

Crochet Hook Sizes

| K | J | I | H | G | F | E | D | 0⁰ | 0 | 1 | 7 | 14 |

Aluminum | Steel

Standard Yarn Sizes

Knitting Worsted

Sport weight Yarn

Rug Yarn

Fingering Yarn

Bulky Yarn

Novelty Yarn

Standard yarn sizes

Most common yarns fit into one of the following categories. The drawings at left show the actual size of each kind of yarn.

Knitting worsted. The heaviest of the standard yarns, this yarn is most commonly used for both knitting and crocheting. Made of wool or manmade fibers, it is usually 4-ply — that is, four single threads twisted together to produce a strong, hard-wearing yarn.

Sport weight yarn. This yarn comes in 3-ply or 4-ply, but either way it's about half the thickness of knitting worsted.

Rug yarn. Thicker and denser than knitting worsted but thinner than bulky yarns, rug yarn is 3-ply and available in cotton or acrylic.

Fingering yarn and baby yarn. Available in both 3-ply and 4-ply, these yarns are thin, soft, and smooth.

Bulky yarns. Either 1, 2, 3, or 4-ply, bulky yarns are much thicker than knitting worsted. The very heavy imported and domestic hand spuns usually fall into this category.

Novelty yarns. Bouclé, chenille, and metallics, a few of the yarns falling into this category, are 1, 2, 3, or 4-ply and come in various weights.

yarns by the ounce, traditional knitting worsted in 2 or 4-ounce skeins. The following suggestions will help when you're choosing your yarn.

• Beginning crocheters might want to buy their materials at a good yarn shop or a large store with a needlework department specializing in knitting and crochet. These shops usually offer invaluable free advice that can help initially when you're selecting yarn and later if questions or problems arise. When you purchase yarn, ask if someone is available for this kind of consultation.

• Check to see what kind of yarn the pattern calls for. Determine why the designer felt that that yarn was appropriate for the project.

• Consider how a garment will be worn. If it's a sweater, will it be worn alone or under a jacket or coat? Will it be for warmth or just a decorative layer, such as a thin vest?

• Consider maintenance of the piece. A baby blanket should be machine washable, but an evening shawl can be made of a delicate wool that must be dry cleaned. Check labels for care and washing and drying instructions.

• Check the dye lot number on *each* package of yarn to be sure that all dye lot numbers are the same. Buy enough yarn of one dye lot to complete your piece.

• Consider quality. In most instances, you *do* get what you pay for. So decide if an expensive wool will serve your purposes better (and essentially be a better value for your money) than a cheap yarn that will, at best, do only an adequate job. Remember that most yarns can be unraveled and reused. (Mohair is an exception; it tangles easily.) See page 31 for information on reusing yarn.

• Last — and very important: Select a yarn that you will enjoy working with for the entire project, one that will please you every time you touch it, one that you will admire when looking at the finished product.

Kinds of yarns

Crochet can be worked with a continuous strand of almost anything, from the most luxurious yarn to plain string. Here are some of the most popular materials.

Wool, available in any weight, texture, ply, and color, is the most versatile of all materials. Generally, it takes a little more care than the synthetics, but it's also much warmer. A word of caution — some people are allergic to wool.

Cotton comes in many weights, is washable (check to see if it has been preshrunk), dyeable, and comfortable. It is less expensive than wool, does not wear as well as synthetics or wool, and generally has very little stretch.

Linen is strong and also has very little stretch. It has a distinctive "look" that cannot be duplicated with a synthetic yarn. It is washable.

Synthetics and mixtures (including rayon, orlon, nylon, acrylic, and acetate) are washable (they will not shrink), non-allergenic, and mothproof. These qualities make them a natural choice for such projects as baby blankets, children's clothes, and the hammock shown on page 59.

Unusual media might include leather thongs, macramé cord, raffia, jute, rope, nylon tubing, or any continuous strand of material that suits your fancy. When working with rope or jute, you may want to protect your hands with gloves.

Miscellaneous Supplies

Probably you'll want to have at hand a few other supplies to complement your yarn and hooks:
- Small metal ruler and tape measure
- Small scissors for snipping yarn
- Yarn needle or weaver for weaving in tail ends
- Toothbrush holder, small box, or bag to hold hooks
- Commercial markers, paper clips, or safety pins
- Blocking supplies (see page 32)
- Hook sizer
- Basket, tote bag, or knitting bag to hold your work
- Yarn winder and swift. (Although these tools are not absolutely necessary, you might want to consider investing in them, particularly if you want to experiment with unusual yarns that are sold by the pound instead of in the neatly packaged pull-skeins. The swift expands like an umbrella to hold any size hank of yarn. The yarn winder quickly turns the yarn into a tidy cone or ball.)

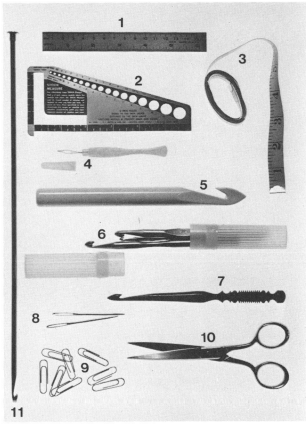

Miscellaneous supplies *include 1) metal ruler, 2) hook sizer, 3) tape measure, 4) yarn weaver, 5) jumbo hook, 6) toothbrush holder and hooks, 7) handmade hook, 8) yarn needles, 9) paper clips, 10) scissors, 11) afghan hook.*

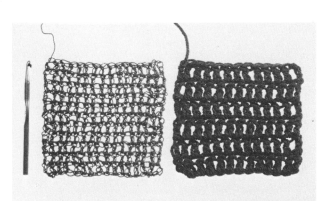

See the difference *yarn size makes in gauge: with fingering yarn (left), 5½ rows = 2 inches; with rug yarn (right), 3 rows = 2 inches. Both swatches were crocheted with the same hook (size K) and the same stitch (double crochet).*

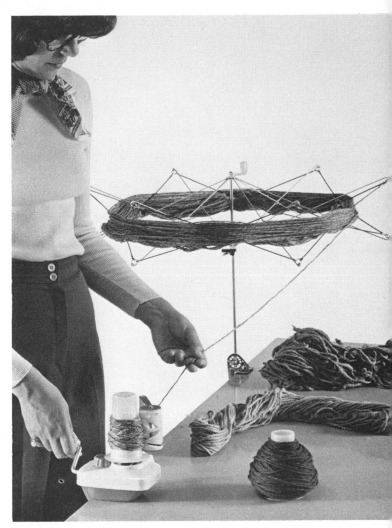

Umbrellalike yarn swift *holds skein of yarn and rotates as yarn is pulled off and turned into a ball by yarn winder.*

Teach yourself *the basic stitches by following the directions in this chapter and making a sample swatch. The one above has several rows of single crochet and 11 rows of double crochet. The hook is held in the knife position.*

Learning the Basic Stitches

from single to double triple

Learning to crochet is like learning to do anything else: it takes a little patience and, of course, practice. Begin by working up sample swatches of the basic stitches, using an inexpensive but conventional yarn (such as knitting worsted) and a fairly large aluminum hook (such as H, I, or J).

Consider the first few hours and your first swatches as strictly practice. Don't worry about being perfect — chances are you'll pull out the swatches and reuse the yarn.

Try to get a good feeling for working with yarn. Relax; let your own rhythm develop. After some practice, you'll find crocheting a very relaxing and almost automatic hobby. In fact, it will become so natural you'll feel lost without it when you sit down to watch television or chat with a friend.

Stitches at a glance

The chain stitch — the simplest stitch of all — serves as the foundation row. The slip stitch and single crochet are the most basic stitches. Variations of these are double and triple crochet, formed by wrapping the yarn around the hook a different number of times.

All crochet begins with a row of chain stitches, followed by a row of single, double, or any other crochet stitch worked into the chains. After all the chains are filled, you turn the work and form a new row by crocheting into the previous row of stitches. (The swatches pictured with each stitch show how each stitch looks when worked in a group.) Because you turn your work each time you start a new row, and because every row is the same stitch, the piece has no right or wrong side. Occasionally this rule is broken — when you repeatedly change colors or when you work a special pattern stitch.

Experimenting with hooks and yarns

After you've mastered some of the basic stitches, try using different hooks and yarns. For example, double crochet worked with a large hook and small yarn displays a different character than double crochet worked with a large hook and large yarn (see photo, page 9). By becoming familiar with the effects created by various combinations of yarns, hooks, and stitches, you will be able to visualize patterns when reading through crochet instructions.

Moods, tension, and gauge

As you practice the basic stitches, you should be aware of, but not overly concerned with, how tightly or loosely you crochet. However, when crocheting a project, be sure you work to the gauge given, or the size of your piece will be off. (For a complete discussion of gauge, see page 29.)

You'll probably be surprised to learn that the size and tightness of your stitches can be affected by your mood. On a tense day, your stitches will be tight, for the yarn won't slip through your fingers as easily as on a relaxed, breezy day. Usually people start out with a tight crochet, getting looser and more even as they work. To compensate for uneven crochet, start with a bigger-than-usual hook, then switch to a smaller one as you loosen up. Check the size of your stitches by measuring them with a ruler.

The Language of Crochet

Crochet instructions are written in a kind of shorthand. When you first learn to crochet, the instructions may seem very foreign to you, but in no time at all you'll be thinking in the language of crochet.

Below are the abbreviated terms you'll be using:

beg: beginning

ch(s): chain(s) or chain stitch

cl: cluster

dc: double crochet

dec(s): decrease(s)

dtr: double triple crochet

hdc: half double crochet

inc(s): increase(s)

lp(s): loop(s)

pat: pattern

rep: repeat

rnd: round

sc: single crochet

sk: skip

sl st: slip stitch

sp(s): space(s)

st(s): stitch(es)

tog: together

tr: triple crochet

yo: yarn over hook

*: repeat directions from asterisk as many times as specified.

x: times (see page 29 for a complete explanation).

( ): repeat directions in parentheses as many times as specified (see page 29 for a complete explanation).

Basic Stitches:

Right-Handed

On the next seven pages are step-by-step instructions for learning to crochet if you are right-handed. For left-hand instructions, turn to page 20.

If you wish to make a sampler of the stitches, see page 31 for how to end off.

(A listing of crochet abbreviations is on page 11.)

Holding the hook and yarn

You can hold the crochet hook two ways. Both methods have loyal supporters who say that theirs is the best way. You'll have to try both and decide which is more comfortable for you.

• Knife position. Hold the hook between thumb and forefinger as you would a knife. Rest the bottom of the hook lightly on the other fingers.

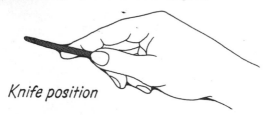

Knife position

• Pencil position. Hold the hook between thumb and forefinger as you would a pencil, with thumb and forefinger on the flat part of the hook, and keep your middle finger forward to rest near the tip. Though this position gives you more control of the hook, it won't make your crocheting more efficient if it isn't comfortable for you.

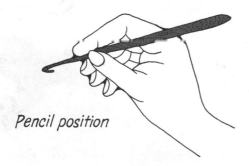

Pencil position

With your left hand, weave the yarn from the ball through your fingers as shown in either of the sketches below. Remember that the yarn always comes *over* your forefinger, from back to front, so that you can control its movement with your forefinger. You want the yarn to feed easily from the ball to the work with a consistent tension.

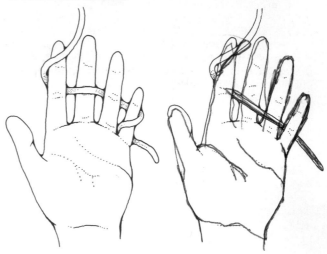

Use the middle finger and thumb of your left hand to hold the stitches you have made.

Counting stitches

Counting the number of stitches you have completed is more difficult in crochet than in knitting because the stitches are not left on the hook (the afghan stitch is an exception). The numbers under the single crochet stitches in the illustration below will help you understand how to count them individually.

A basic rule for crochet

For all stitches (except the afghan stitch), *always* insert the hook under the two top loops of the previous stitch unless otherwise specified.

Slip Knot

You need to make a slip knot to hold your hook.
1) Several inches in from the end of yarn, make a loop. Hold top of loop between thumb and forefinger with left hand.
2) Place long yarn end behind loop and pull yarn through loop with hook **[A].**
3) Pull yarn ends to tighten loop **[B].**

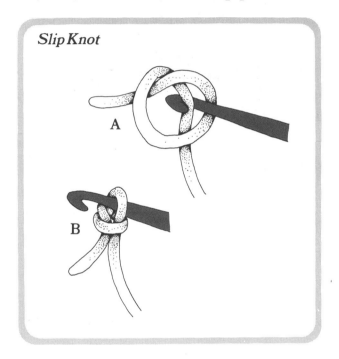

Slip Knot

Chain Stitch

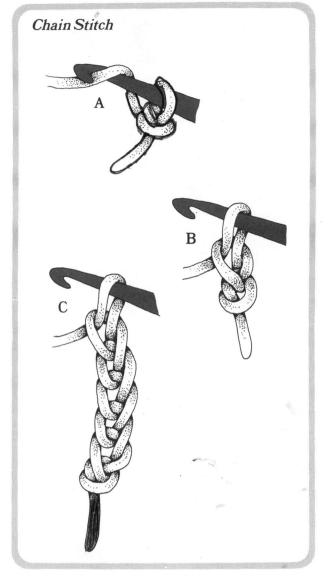

Chain Stitch (ch)

This simple stitch forms the foundation on which all crochet builds. Practice it (make a chain of 100 stitches or more) to gain a feeling for it and to develop stitches that are evenly sized and spaced. After you feel comfortable with the chain stitch, make a row of 20 chains to use as a base for the rest of your stitches.
1) Insert hook into slip knot.
2) Wrap yarn around hook clockwise, catching yarn on hook **[A].** This is referred to as "yarn over hook" (yo).
3) Pull yarn through loop (lp) on hook **[B].** The yo and pulling of yarn through the lp on hook completes one chain stitch (ch).
4) Repeat (rep) steps 2 and 3 until ch is desired length **[C].** As you work, keep thumb and middle finger of left hand near the newest stitch to keep the ch from twisting.

Chain stitch

Single Crochet (sc)

Shortest of the basic stitches, single crochet is a tight stitch that produces a flat design.

1) Make a chain (ch) of any length (about 20 is good for a practice swatch).

2) Insert hook under two top loops (lps) of 2nd ch from hook.

3) Yarn over hook (yo) **[A]**, pull yarn through lp on hook (2 lps remain on hook) **[B]**.

4) Yo and pull yarn through 2 lps on hook. You have completed one sc **[C]**.

5) Insert hook into next ch, repeat (rep) steps 3 and 4. Work to end of row, ch 1 (always ch 1 at end of every sc row, except the very last row of your piece) **[D]**.

6) Turn work (from right to left so yarn remains at back) to start next row **[E]**.

7) On subsequent rows, insert hook in 1st stitch (st) of previous row **[F]**. Rep steps 3 and 4 to complete one sc in each st of previous row. Ch 1, turn.

Single crochet

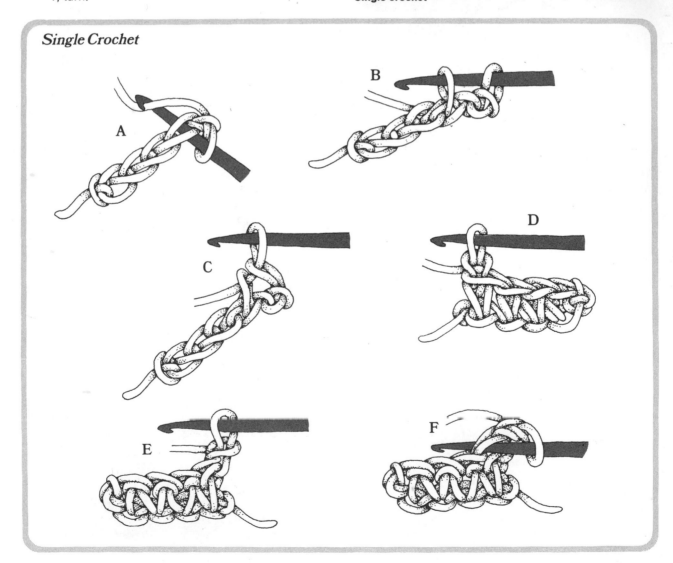

Single Crochet

A B C D E F

Double Crochet (dc)

Double crochet is twice the height of single crochet and a little looser.

1) Make a chain (ch) of any length.
2) Yarn over hook (yo), insert hook in 4th ch from hook. (The 3 skipped chs will be referred to as the "turning ch.")
3) Yo **[A]** and pull yarn through lp (3 lps on hook) **[B]**.
4) Yo and pull yarn through 2 lps (2 lps on hook) **[C]**.
5) Yo and pull yarn through 2 lps on hook. You have completed one dc **[D]**.
6) Yo and insert hook in next ch. Repeat (rep) steps 3-5, making a dc in each ch across.
7) At end of row, ch 3 and turn work from right to left so yarn remains at back **[E]**.
8) The ch-3 is counted as the 1st dc of the next row. Skip (sk) 1st st, dc in next (2nd) dc, inserting hook under 2 top strands **[F]**. Work a dc in each dc to end. The last dc in row is worked in top of turning ch of previous row **[G]**. Ch 3, turn.

Double crochet

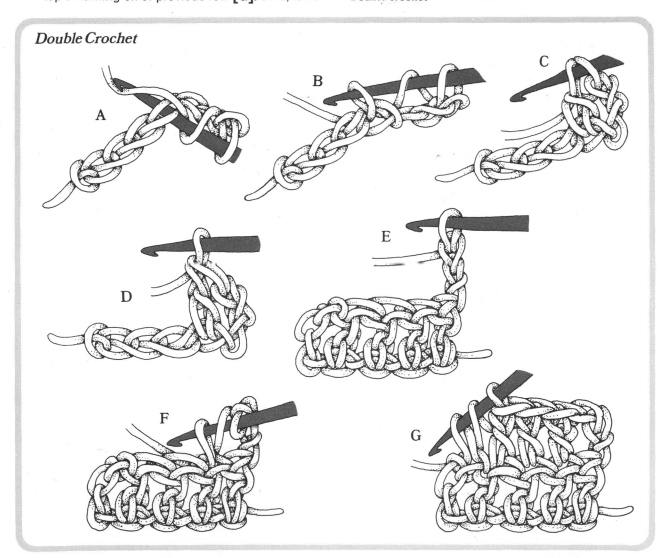

Double Crochet

Half Double Crochet (hdc)

Half double is taller than single crochet but not as tall as double crochet. With half double, a definite chain shows at the top of the work; with all other crochet stitches, the chain shows only on one side.

1) Make a chain (ch) of any length.
2) Yarn over hook (yo) and insert hook into 3rd ch from hook **[A]**.
3) Yo and pull yarn through lp (3 lps on hook) **[B]**.
4) Yo and pull yarn through the 3 lps on hook. You have completed one hdc **[C]**.
5) Yo and insert hook into next ch. Repeat (rep) steps 3-4 and work a hdc in each ch across row. Ch 2 **[D]**, turn.
6) On succeeding rows, yo and insert hook under the 2 strands on top in 1st st (in hdc, turning ch doesn't count as 1st hdc). Rep steps 3 and 4.

Half double crochet

Half Double Crochet

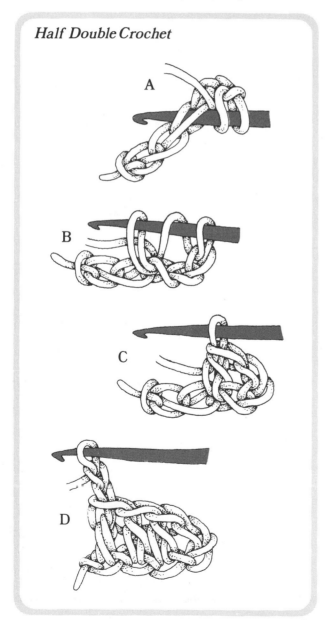

Slip Stitch (sl st)

Slip stitch is a joining stitch. Shorter than a single crochet, it can join a chain to form a ring, finish a round off smoothly (to eliminate a spiral effect on a round piece when one round ends and the next begins), or strengthen a finished piece and keep it from stretching. Slip stitch is never used alone.

To form a slip stitch, working off a chain or with a swatch of single, half double, or double crochet, insert hook into 1st stitch (st), yarn over hook (yo), pull yarn through st and loop (lp) on hook (1 lp on hook). Continue across row in this manner. Since slip stitch is generally used to end a piece, you won't chain or turn at the end of the row, but will tie off. Specific instructions will be given if you need to turn.

To form a ring, make a ch, insert hook in first ch made, yo **[A]**, and pull yarn through both ch and lp on hook.

To Form a Ring

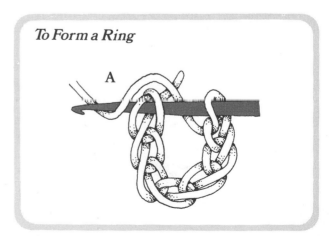

Increases and Decreases in the Basic Stitches

"Increasing" and "decreasing" widen and narrow areas and provide shaping. Increasing is less complicated than decreasing. You simply work two stitches in the same stitch of the previous row, or you add a stitch at the beginning or end of a row in the turning chain. Which increase method to use is given with directions for each project.

Although the method for decreasing varies with each stitch, basically you are joining several stitches into one stitch.

Single crochet decrease. 1) Insert hook in next sc, yo, pull yarn through 1 lp (2 lps now on hook). Insert hook in next sc, yo, pull yarn through 1 lp (3 lps on hook). **2)** Yo **[A]** and pull yarn through all 3 lps. You have made a dec by working 2 sc together.

Double crochet decrease. 1) Yo, insert hook in next dc, yo, pull yarn through (3 lps on hook). **2)** Yo, pull yarn through 2 lps (2 lps on hook). **3)** Yo, insert hook in next st, yo, pull yarn through (4 lps on hook). **4)** Yo, pull yarn through 2 lps (3 lps on hook). **5)** Yo **[A]**, pull yarn through the 3 lps. You have made a dec by working 2 dc together.

Decreasing in other stitches. Shaping is rarely used in longer stitches; if it is, specific directions are given in the instructions for the garment. As a rule of thumb, you can decrease by working two stitches together (increase the number of loops on the hook) or by skipping the first stitch or the next-to-last stitch in a row.

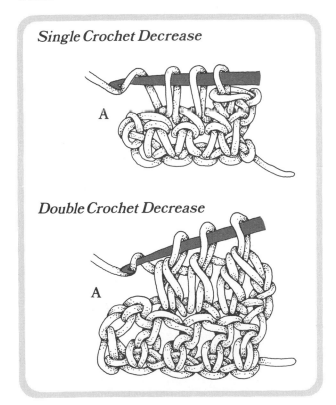

Single Crochet Decrease

A

Double Crochet Decrease

A

Triple Crochet (tr)

Triple crochet is taller than double crochet and produces a loose, more open stitch. It isn't used as frequently as single or double crochet.
1) Make a chain (ch) of any length.
2) Yarn over hook (yo) twice, insert hook into 5th ch from hook.
3) Yo, pull yarn through loop (4 lps on hook) **[A]**.
4) Yo, pull yarn through 2 lps on hook (3 lps on hook).
5) Yo, pull yarn through 2 lps on hook 2 more times (1 lp on hook). You have completed one tr **[B]**.
6) Yo twice, insert hook into next ch. Repeat (rep) steps 3-5 and work a tr in each ch across to end of row. Ch 4, turn.
7) On the next rows, insert hook into 2nd st. The turning ch is the first tr of next row. Work last tr of row in 4th turning ch of previous row. Ch 4, turn.

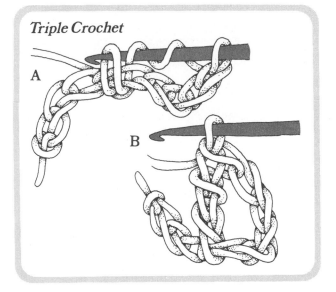

Triple Crochet

A

B

Triple crochet

Double Triple (dtr)

Double triple is one stitch taller than triple crochet.
1) Make a chain (ch) of any length.
2) Yarn over hook (yo) 3 times, insert hook into 6th ch from hook.
3) Yo, pull yarn through loop (5 lps on hook) **[A]**.
4) Yo and pull yarn through 2 lps at a time, 4 times. You have completed one dtr **[B]**.
5) Yo 3 times, insert hook in next ch, repeat (rep) steps 3-4 and work to end of row, ch 5, turn.
6) Yo 3 times, insert hook into 2nd st of next row. Rep steps 3 and 4.

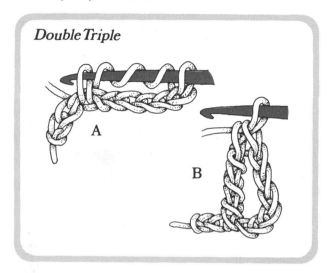

Double Triple

Double triple crochet

Afghan Stitch

In a class by itself, the afghan stitch is worked with a different hook and resembles a knitting stitch more than a crochet stitch. (It is sometimes called "Tunisian crochet.") The hook holds a whole row of stitches that are then worked off the hook one by one. Though it takes two rows to complete the afghan stitch, the two rows are referred to as row 1 (first half) and row 1 (second half).

The completed work has an obvious front and back, formed by the "pick up" row (first half) and the "stitch" row (second half). You don't turn your work; instead, you work back and forth on the same side of the piece.
1) Using an afghan hook, make a chain (ch) of any length.
2) *Row 1, first half or "pick-up row":* Skip (sk) 1st ch, insert hook under top strand *only* of next ch, yarn over hook (yo), pull yarn through ch (2 lps on hook). Repeat in each ch across row, leaving all loops (lps) on hook **[A]**. *Row 1, second half or "stitch row":* yo, pull yarn through 1st lp on hook * yo, pull yarn through 2 lps, rep from * across **[B]**. The remaining lp serves as the first st of the next row. If you look carefully at this row, you will see that you have a series of upright (or vertical) stitches called "bars."
3) *Row 2, first half:* Insert hook under 2nd vertical bar **[C]**, yo, pull yarn through lp. Rep for each bar across, keeping all lps on hook. To end row, insert hook under last bar and the st directly behind it, yo, pull yarn through a lp **[D]**. *Row 2, second half:* rep stitch row in step 2.
4) Rep row 2 for afghan pattern. To end your piece, work a sl st in each bar across.

Increase for afghan stitch. (Always done on first half of stitch row.) Insert hook into ch between the next 2 vertical bars, yo, pull yarn through a lp. Insert hook under next vertical bar, yo, pull through lp **[E]**.

Decrease for afghan stitch. Insert hook under the next 2 vertical bars, yo, pull yarn through a lp **[F]**.

Points to remember. 1) When working the afghan stitch, never turn your piece. You work down the row on the right side, then back on the same (right) side of your work. **2)** Always begin the second half of a row by pulling yarn through one stitch only. After you've completed the first stitch, then pull through two stitches at a time. **3)** The last stitch remaining on the hook is always the first stitch of the next row. **4)** Always skip the first bar when starting a row. **5)** Unless you increase or decrease, you will always be working with exactly the same number of stitches as established on the chain. **6)** Increases and decreases are worked only in the first half of the stitch row.

Afghan stitch

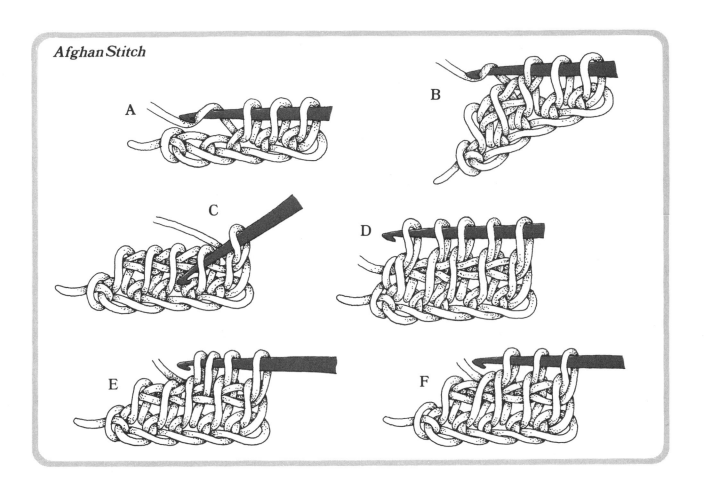

Afghan Stitch

A

B

C

D

E

F

How to Turn Work

Each stitch calls for a certain number of chains to be worked at the end of each row. The reason is that, since the chain stitches are the same length as the stitch you're doing, they bring you up to the height of the next row of stitches.

Here is a listing of the number of chains required to start a new row of each stitch:

Stitch	After the row of chains, turn and begin in	At the end of each row,	To begin next row, insert hook in
slip stitch (sl st)	2nd ch from hook	ch 1, turn	1st st
single crochet (sc)	2nd ch from hook	ch 1, turn	1st st
half double (hdc)	3rd ch from hook	ch 2, turn	1st st
double crochet (dc)	4th ch from hook	ch 3, turn	2nd st
triple (tr)	5th ch from hook	ch 4, turn	2nd st
double triple (dtr)	6th ch from hook	ch 5, turn	2nd st

Basic Stitches:

Left-Handed

On the next seven pages are step-by-step instructions for learning to crochet if you are left-handed. For right-hand instructions, turn to page 12.

If you wish to make a sampler of the stitches, see page 31 for how to end off.

(A listing of crochet abbreviations is on page 11.)

Holding the hook and yarn

You can hold the crochet hook two ways. Both methods have loyal supporters who say that theirs is the best way. You'll have to try both and decide which is more comfortable for you.

• Knife position. Hold the hook between thumb and forefinger as you would a knife. Rest the bottom of the hook lightly on the other fingers.

Knife position

• Pencil position. Hold the hook between thumb and forefinger as you would a pencil, with thumb and forefinger on the flat part of the hook, and keep your middle finger forward to rest near the tip. Though this position gives you more control of the hook, it won't make your crocheting more efficient if it isn't comfortable for you.

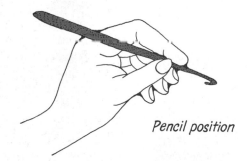

Pencil position

With your right hand, weave the yarn from the ball through your fingers as shown in either of the sketches below. Remember that the yarn always comes *over* your forefinger, from back to front, so that you can control its movement with your forefinger. You want the yarn to feed easily from the ball to the work with a consistent tension.

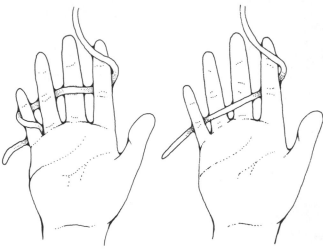

Use the middle finger and thumb of your right hand to hold the stitches you have made.

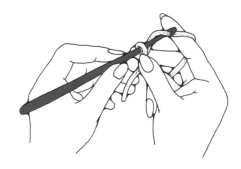

Counting stitches

Counting the number of stitches you have completed is more difficult in crochet than in knitting because the stitches are not left on the hook (the afghan stitch is an exception). The numbers under the single crochet stitches in the illustration below will help you understand how to count them individually.

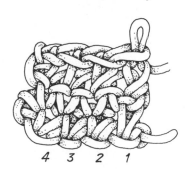

4 3 2 1

A basic rule for crochet

For all stitches (except the afghan stitch), *always* insert the hook under the two top loops of the previous stitch unless otherwise specified.

Slip Knot

You need to make a slip knot to hold your hook.
1) Several inches in from the end of yarn, make a loop. Hold top of loop between thumb and forefinger with right hand.
2) Place long yarn end behind loop and pull yarn through loop with hook **[A].**
3) Pull yarn ends to tighten loop **[B].**

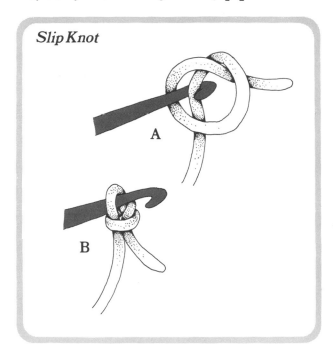

Slip Knot

A

B

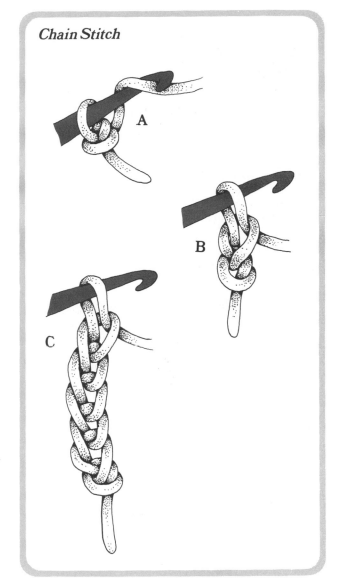

Chain Stitch

A

B

C

Chain Stitch (ch)

This simple stitch forms the foundation on which all crochet builds. Practice it (make a chain of 100 stitches or more) to gain a feeling for it and to develop stitches that are evenly sized and spaced. After you feel comfortable with the chain stitch, make a row of 20 chains to use as a base for the rest of your stitches.
1) Insert hook into slip knot.
2) Wrap yarn around hook clockwise, catching yarn on hook **[A].** This is referred to as "yarn over hook" (yo).
3) Pull yarn through loop (lp) on hook **[B].** The yo and pulling of yarn through the lp on hook completes one chain stitch (ch).
4) Repeat (rep) steps 2 and 3 until ch is desired length **[C].** As you work, keep thumb and middle finger of right hand near the newest stitch to keep the ch from twisting.

Chain stitch

Single Crochet (sc)

Shortest of the basic stitches, single crochet is a tight stitch that produces a flat design.

1) Make a chain (ch) of any length (about 20 is good for a practice swatch).
2) Insert hook under two top loops (lps) of 2nd ch from hook.
3) Yarn over hook (yo) **[A]**, pull yarn through lp on hook (2 lps remain on hook) **[B]**.
4) Yo and pull yarn through 2 lps on hook. You have completed one sc **[C]**.
5) Insert hook into next ch, repeat (rep) steps 3 and 4. Work to end of row, ch 1 (always ch 1 at end of every sc row, except the very last row of your piece **[D]**.
6) Turn work (from left to right so yarn remains at back) to start next row **[E]**.
7) On subsequent rows, insert hook in 1st stitch (st) of previous row **[F]**. Rep steps 3 and 4 to complete one sc in each st of previous row. Ch 1, turn.

Single crochet

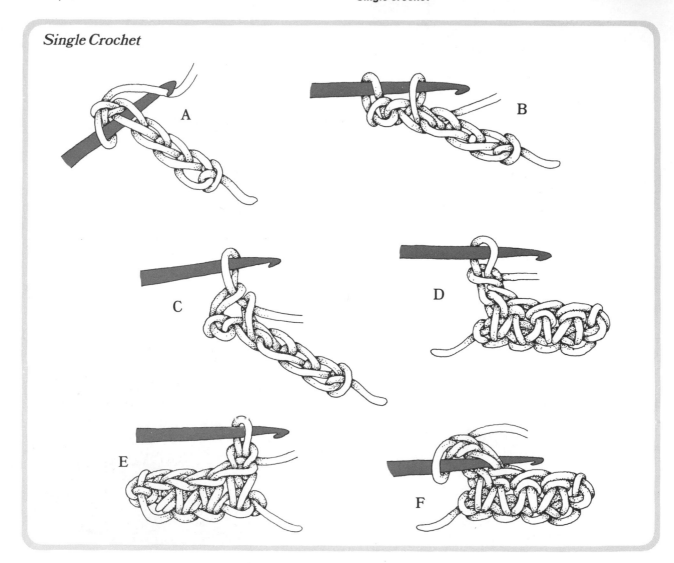

Single Crochet

A

B

C

D

E

F

Double Crochet (dc)

Double crochet is twice the height of a single crochet and a little looser.

1) Make a chain (ch) of any length.
2) Yarn over hook (yo), insert hook in 4th ch from hook. (The 3 skipped chs will be referred to as the "turning ch.")
3) Yo **[A]** and pull yarn through lp (3 lps on hook) **[B]**.
4) Yo and pull yarn through 2 lps (2 lps on hook) **[C]**.
5) Yo and pull yarn through 2 lps on hook. You have completed one dc **[D]**.
6) Yo and insert hook in next ch. Repeat (rep) steps 3-5, making a dc in each ch across.
7) At end of row, ch 3 and turn work from left to right so yarn remains at back **[E]**.
8) The ch-3 is counted as the 1st dc of the next row. Skip (sk) 1st st, dc in next (2nd) dc, inserting hook under 2 top strands **[F]**. Work a dc in each dc to end. The last dc in row is worked in top of turning ch of previous row **[G]**. Ch 3, turn.

Double crochet

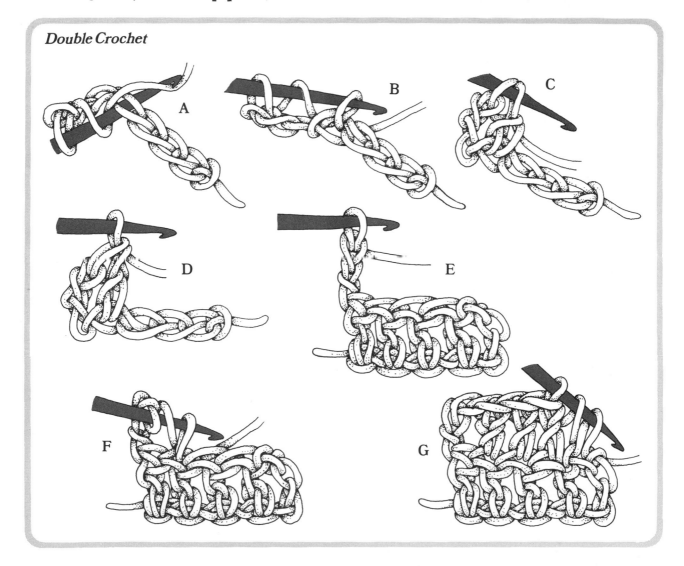

Double Crochet

Half Double Crochet (hdc)

Half double is taller than single crochet but not as tall as double crochet. With half double, a definite chain shows at the top of the work; with all other crochet stitches, the chain shows only on one side.

1) Make a chain (ch) of any length.
2) Yarn over hook (yo) and insert hook into 3rd ch from hook **[A]**.
3) Yo and pull yarn through loop (3 loops on hook) **[B]**.
4) Yo and pull yarn through the 3 lps on hook. You have completed one hdc **[C]**.
5) Yo and insert hook into next ch. Repeat (rep) steps 3-4 and work a hdc in each ch across row. Ch 2 **[D]**, turn.
6) On succeeding rows, yo and insert hook under the 2 strands on top in 1st st (in hdc, turning ch doesn't count as 1st hdc). Rep steps 3 and 4.

Half double crochet

Half Double Crochet

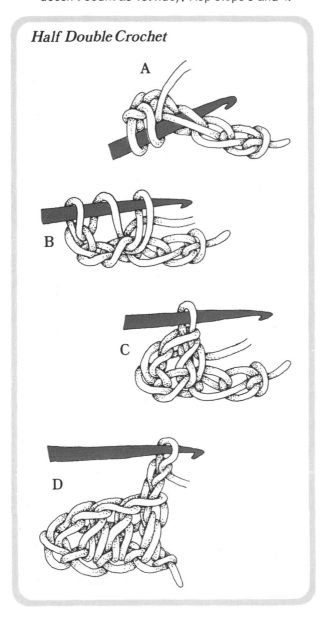

A

B

C

D

Slip Stitch (sl st)

Slip stitch is a joining stitch. Shorter than a single crochet, it can join a chain to form a ring, finish a round off smoothly (to eliminate a spiral effect on a round piece when one round ends and the next begins), or strengthen a finished piece and keep it from stretching. Slip stitch is never used alone.

To form a slip stitch, working with a swatch of single, half double, or double crochet (instead of a chain), insert hook into 1st stitch (st), yarn over hook (yo), pull yarn through st and loop (lp) on hook (1 lp on hook). Continue across row in this manner. Since slip stitch is generally used to end a piece, you won't chain or turn at the end of the row, but will tie off. Specific instructions will be given if you need to turn.

To form a ring, make a ch, insert hook in first ch made, yo **[A],** and pull yarn through both ch and lp on hook.

To Form a Ring

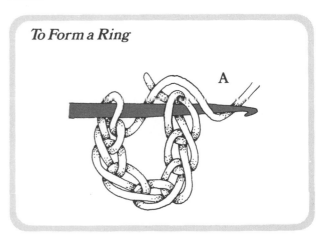

A

Increases and Decreases in the Basic Stitches

"Increasing" and "decreasing" widen and narrow areas and provide shaping. Increasing is less complicated than decreasing. You simply work two stitches in the same stitch of the previous row, or you add a stitch at the beginning or end of a row in the turning chain. Which increase method to use is given with directions for each project.

Although the method for decreasing varies with each stitch, basically you are joining several stitches into one stitch.

Single crochet decrease. 1) Insert hook in next sc, yo, pull yarn through 1 lp (2 lps now on hook). Insert hook in next sc, yo, pull yarn through 1 lp (3 lps on hook). **2)** Yo **[A]** and pull yarn through all 3 lps. You have made a dec by working 2 sc together.

Double crochet decrease. 1) Yo, insert hook in next dc, yo, pull yarn through (3 lps on hook). **2)** Yo, pull yarn through 2 lps (2 lps on hook). **3)** Yo, insert hook in next st, yo, pull yarn through (4 lps on hook). **4)** Yo, pull yarn through 2 lps (3 lps on hook). **5)** Yo **[A]**, pull yarn through the 3 lps. You have made a dec by working 2 dc together.

Decreasing in other stitches. Shaping is rarely used in longer stitches; if it is, specific directions are given in the instructions for the garment. As a rule of thumb, you can decrease by working two stitches together (increase the number of loops on the hook) or by skipping the first stitch or the next-to-last stitch in a row.

Triple Crochet (tr)

Triple crochet is taller than double crochet and produces a looser, more open stitch. It is not used as frequently as single or double crochet.

1) Make a chain (ch) of any length.
2) Yarn over hook (yo) twice, insert hook into 5th ch from hook.
3) Yo, pull yarn through loop (4 lps on hook) **[A]**.
4) Yo, pull yarn through 2 lps on hook (3 lps on hook).
5) Yo, pull yarn through 2 lps on hook 2 more times (1 lp on hook). You have completed one tr **[B]**.
6) Yo twice, insert hook into next ch. Repeat (rep) steps 3-5 and work a tr in each ch across to end of row. Ch 4, turn.
7) On the next rows, insert hook into 2nd st. The turning ch is the first tr of next row. Work last tr of row in 4th turning ch of previous row. Ch 4, turn.

Triple Crochet

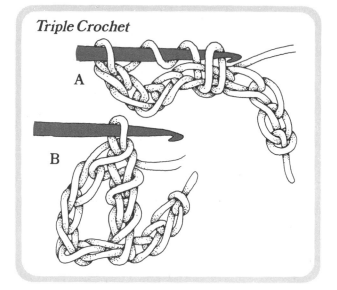

Single Crochet Decrease

Double Crochet Decrease

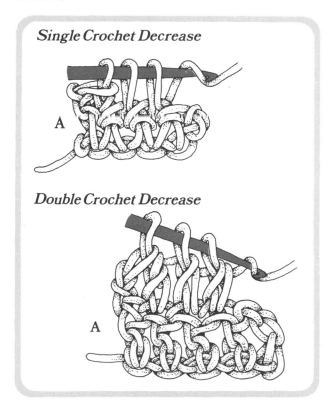

Triple crochet

Double Triple (dtr)

Double triple is one stitch taller than triple crochet.
1) Make a chain (ch) of any length.
2) Yarn over hook (yo) 3 times, insert hook into 6th ch from hook.
3) Yo, pull yarn through loop (5 lps on hook) **[A]**.
4) Yo and pull yarn through 2 lps at a time, 4 times. You have completed one dtr **[B]**.
5) Yo 3 times, insert hook in next ch, repeat (rep) steps 3-4 and work to end of row, ch 5, turn.
6) Yo 3 times, insert hook into 2nd st of next row. Rep steps 3 and 4.

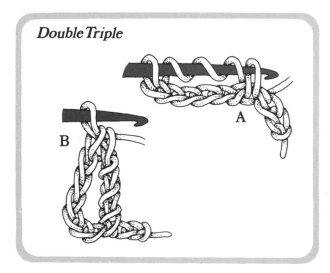

Double Triple

Double triple crochet

Afghan Stitch

In a class by itself, the afghan stitch is worked with a different hook and resembles a knitting stitch more than a crochet stitch. (It is sometimes called "Tunisian crochet.") The hook holds a whole row of stitches that are then worked off the hook one by one. Though it takes two rows to complete the afghan stitch, the two rows are referred to as row 1 (first half) and row 1 (second half).

The completed work has an obvious front and back, formed by the "pick up" row (first half) and the "stitch" row (second half). You don't turn your work; instead, you work back and forth on the same side of the piece.
1) Using an afghan hook, make a chain (ch) of any length.
2) *Row 1, first half or "pick-up row":* Skip (sk) 1st ch, insert hook under top strand *only* of next ch, yarn over hook (yo), pull yarn through ch (2 lps on hook). Repeat in each ch across row, leaving all loops (lps) on hook **[A]**. *Row 1, second half or "stitch row":* yo, pull yarn through 1st lp on hook, * yo, pull yarn through 2 lps, rep from * across **[B]**. The remaining lp serves as the first st of the next row. If you look carefully at this row, you will see that you have a series of upright (or vertical) stitches called "bars."
3) *Row 2, first half:* Insert hook under 2nd vertical bar **[C]**, yo, pull yarn through lp. Rep for each bar across, keeping all lps on hook. To end row, insert hook under last bar and the st directly behind it, yo, pull yarn through a lp **[D]**. *Row 2, second half:* rep stitch row in step 2.
4) Rep row 2 for afghan pattern. To end your piece, work a sl st in each bar across.

Increase for afghan stitch. (Always done on first half of stitch row.) Insert hook into ch between the next 2 vertical bars, yo, pull yarn through a lp. Insert hook under next vertical bar, yo, pull through lp **[E]**.

Decrease for afghan stitch. Insert hook under the next 2 vertical bars, yo, pull yarn through lp **[F]**.

Points to remember. 1) When working the afghan stitch, never turn your piece. You work down the row on the right side, then back on the same (right) side of your work. **2)** Always begin the second half of a row by pulling yarn through one stitch only. After you've completed the first stitch, then pull through two stitches at a time. **3)** The last stitch remaining on the hook is always the first stitch of the next row. **4)** Always skip the first bar when starting a row. **5)** Unless you increase or decrease, you will always be working with exactly the same number of stitches as established in the chain. **6)** Increases and decreases are worked only in the first half of the stitch row.

Afghan stitch

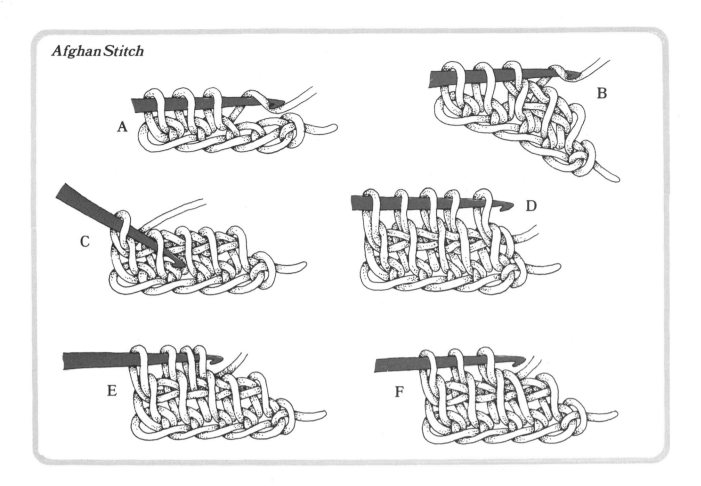

Afghan Stitch

A

B

C

D

E

F

How to Turn Work

Each stitch calls for a certain number of chains to be worked at the end of each row. The reason is that, since the chain stitches are the same length as the stitch you're doing, they bring you up to the height of the next row of stitches.

Here is a listing of the number of chains required to start a new row of each stitch:

Stitch	After the row of chains, turn and begin in	At the end of each row,	To begin next row, insert hook in
slip stitch (sl st)	2nd ch from hook	ch 1, turn	1st st
single crochet (sc)	2nd ch from hook	ch 1, turn	1st st
half double (hdc)	3rd ch from hook	ch 2, turn	1st st
double crochet (dc)	4th ch from hook	ch 3, turn	2nd st
triple (tr)	5th ch from hook	ch 4, turn	2nd st
double triple (dtr)	6th ch from hook	ch 5, turn	2nd st

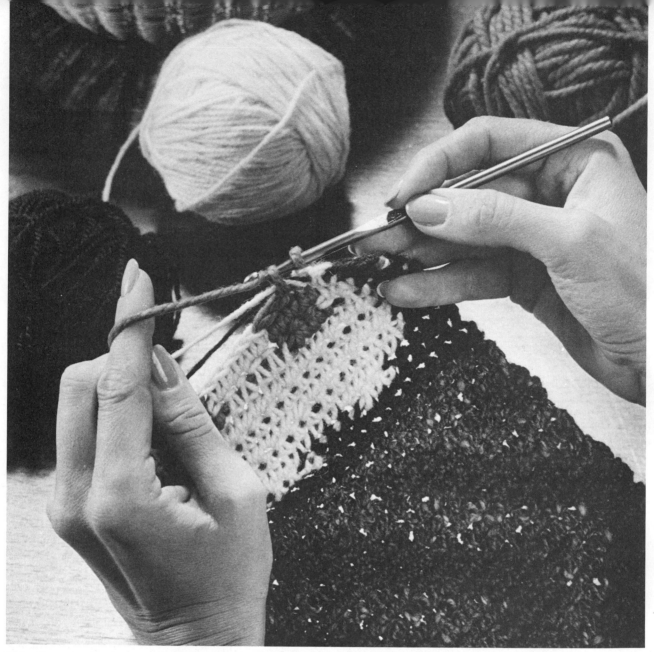

Color-through-color *is an exciting technique to learn and an enjoyable one to use. Extra colors are carried on top of the previous row of stitches and picked up as they are needed. For a detailed explanation, see page 30.*

Crochet Techniques--

patterns, color, finishing, geometric shapes

Now that you've mastered the basic stitches, you'll want to crochet your first piece. But to be able to do this, you'll need to learn some basic techniques, such as how to read a pattern, determine your gauge, change colors and yarns, end your work, and block the finished piece.

For the adventurous we've included information on crocheting geometric shapes. Once you understand the theories involved in making shapes and forms, you can translate them into parts of a garment or anything else you plan to make. For example, a simple pullover sweater is made of three tubes: the two sleeves and the body. If you want a turtleneck collar, add another tube of a smaller dimension. A necktie starts with a simple triangle; placemats, rugs, hammocks are just rectangles.

How to Read a Written Pattern

To read project instructions, such as those on pages 34-69, you have to understand some symbols and terminology. You're already acquainted with the stitch abbreviations, listed in chart form on page 11 for quick reference.

Symbols to watch for

Commas (always pause when you come to one) separate two kinds of stitches. For example, if the instructions say "2 sc, 2 dc," you will work two single crochet stitches in two stitches of the previous row and then two double crochet stitches in the next two stitches of the previous row.

Hyphens refer to a stitch that is already made and that will be used as a base for another procedure. For example, "3 dc in the ch-3 sp" means to make three double crochets in the space left by the group of three chains from the previous row.

Parentheses are used for several purposes:

(5 sc) at the end of a row or round refers to the number of stitches (in this case five single crochets) that you have made in that row or round.

(5 sc, ch 1)5x means to repeat five times that combination of stitches enclosed in the parentheses.

5(6,7)sc indicates a size change, with the numbers in parentheses referring to larger sizes. When parentheses are used this way, exact size changes will be noted in the instructions.

Multiples are designated by an "x" after a combination of stitches enclosed in parentheses (see parentheses discussion above).

Inc evenly means you can choose where to put your increases in that row or round; the only requisite is that they be spaced evenly.

Pattern reading aids

If you have trouble "tracking" a pattern, you may want to use some of the following aids:
• Place a ruler on the page, just below the row you're working on. Move the ruler down after you complete each row. This will keep you from being distracted by subsequent rows.
• Write out each row on an index card and flip the card over after the row is completed. If a pattern is made of a group of rows to be repeated, either put all the rows on one card or put them on separate cards, paper-clipped together.
• Stick large or glass-headed straight pins into the book at the beginning and end of each row (this works particularly well for graphs or color charts). Move the pins down after each row is completed.

Gauge--the Key to Success

Working to the proper gauge is crucial, for that will determine whether your item will be the right size.

Every project in this book gives a gauge, which means the number of stitches and the number of rows you work per inch. If your gauge matches that of the pattern, you'll have the same number of stitches and rows to the inch as the master design, making your piece the same size as the one that you're following.

The size of the hook and yarn and the tension of the yarn determine the gauge. To test your gauge against that of the pattern, take the same size hook and yarn as called for in the instructions and make a 4-inch-square test swatch of the stitch or pattern stitch you'll be using.

Measure the swatch with a ruler, marking a 2-inch-square space with straight pins, as shown below. Count the number of stitches between the 2-inch space and divide by two to get the number of stitches per inch. Repeat this procedure vertically, counting the number of rows between the 2-inch pin markers and dividing by two.

If your swatch doesn't come very close to the number of stitches and rows called for in the pattern, make a second swatch, concentrating on crocheting looser or tighter to achieve the proper gauge. Too many stitches per inch means you were holding the yarn too tightly; too few stitches per inch means you weren't controlling the yarn.

If your second swatch is still off, switch to a larger or smaller hook. Remember, it's not the hook size that is so important — its the proper gauge. Notice that all of our projects call for a certain hook size "or hook to give proper gauge."

If you're crocheting with an unusual yarn, this is the time to check for shrinkage. Wash your swatch by the method you plan to use for your completed piece and remeasure it after it's dry. If it has shrunk a great deal, preshrink the yarn before you begin to crochet.

To check your gauge, *place straight pins 2 inches apart on your test swatch; then count the number of stitches (9 here) between the pins. Repeat the process vertically for the number of rows per inch.*

Determining quantity of yarn needed

When you decide to change greatly a written pattern or design your own, there are several ways to determine how much yarn you'll need. You can use as a guide a project that's similar to the one you'll be making and that calls for the same kind of yarn. Experienced salespeople in yarn shops will also be able to help you estimate amounts. But the most accurate way is to crochet a test swatch.

Buy a small amount of the yarn you plan to use (enough for a 4-inch-square swatch) and note its yardage or weight. If yardage or weight is not known, measure out 20 yards of yarn and crochet a 4-inch-square swatch in the stitch or pattern stitch you'll be using. If you run out of yarn, measure out another 20-yard piece.

When your swatch is completed, subtract the amount of yarn left from the original weight or from the number of yards you began with. Try to approximate how many 4-inch squares it will take to make your garment. Then multiply the number of swatches by the number of yards in each swatch to figure about how much yarn to buy.

At the time you purchase yarn, buy a little extra, making sure it's all from the same dye lot. If you run out of yarn and have to buy more, it'll be impossible to match dye lots. Many shops will let you return unused yarn (whole balls or skeins with wrappers intact, along with your receipt) within a reasonable length of time and will give you credit toward your next purchase. Check with each shop on its return policy before you buy.

Joining Yarn & Color-through-Color

Changing colors can be one of crochet's most exciting techniques, for it transforms a simple pattern into a graphic representation of a scene or abstract design. Two examples are the plain and scenic vests shown on page 42 and the bold afghan shown on page 64.

The technique of changing colors — called "color-through-color," "carrying color along," or "tapestry stitch" — can be used when you're following written color changes or a color chart. The idea is to carry along, as you crochet, all the colors you're using in a row. The extra yarns are placed on top of the stitches of the previous row, and you crochet around them until they are needed.

This same technique is used to join a new strand of yarn of the same color, eliminating the need to weave in the tail end of the old ball of yarn.

To start a new color, simply lay the strand loosely on top of the row of stitches a few stitches before you need it (leave the tail hanging out; you can snip it off later). Work the next stitches in the old color, around the new color as if it were part of the stitches of the previous row. When it's time to introduce the new color, pick it up on the last yarn over of the previous stitch, so that all of the new stitch will be in the new color (see illustrations below). Carry this color loosely so it won't pucker the work.

Repeat this procedure every time you change colors. When you're finished with one of the colors, carry it along for a few stitches to secure it in the work; then snip it off.

Extra colors are hidden best in denser stitches, such as single or half double crochet.

Color charts

A color chart is a stitch-by-stitch and row-by-row breakdown of every color used in a particular pattern or project. With each color chart is a key explaining which color each symbol stands for. As you crochet, add new colors (using the color-through-color technique) as necessary to correspond to the symbols on the chart. (Refer to the color chart on page 44.)

Enlarging a design

Occasionally you'll need to enlarge a design and superimpose it on graph paper (the scenic vest design on page 43 will have to be enlarged this way). A square on the design grid you'll follow will not represent each stitch, such as in a color chart, but will represent several stitches and rows.

To figure out the number of stitches and rows per square on the grid, choose graph paper whose squares per inch equal the stitches per inch in the gauge of the piece you'll be making. (If it's an uneven number of squares per inch, you may have to make your own graph.)

Each square on the grid you're enlarging represents a certain number of inches. Transfer every grid square to your graph paper, duplicating the number of squares per inch. Then, on the graph paper, draw a rectangle of the same shape as the original grid. You will now have an actual size replica of the original rectangle or square.

Within the rectangle, make tiny marks on each

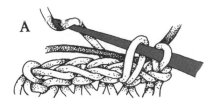

To add a new color, *lay yarn strand loosely on top of row of stitches before you need it (see illustration A). Crochet the next few stitches using old color. At appropriate place, add the new color on last yarn over of previous stitch (see illustrations B and C).*

square of the graph paper, duplicating the outline of the design you're copying. Connect the marks by sketching in the outline.

Use colored pencils or crayons to indicate color changes or make a key with symbols to represent each color. Proceed as in "Color Charts" (page 30).

Ending a Piece

When you're ready to end your piece or test swatch, simply cut the yarn, leaving an end about 3 inches long. Yarn over and pull the loose end all the way through last loop on hook (see illustration A). Thread loose end through a yarn needle and weave it into the second-to-last row of stitches in the back of the stitches (see illustration B). Once the yarn end is secure, snip off the remaining "tail."

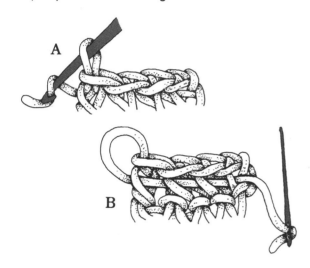

Joining Two Pieces of Crochet

Some crochet projects, such as a cardigan sweater, are worked in pieces and must be joined. You have several choices of how to do this. No matter which method you use, be sure to work loosely — seams must have some room to stretch.

Slip stitch. Pin pieces together. Wrong sides facing each other will give a ridge of slip stitch on the right side of your work; right sides facing each other will put the ridge on the inside of the work. Insert hook into top loops of both pieces and make a slip stitch (see page 16 or 24). Work loosely and continue across row, catching loops of both pieces.

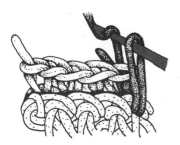

Single crochet. Pin pieces with right sides together. Insert hook into top loops of both pieces and work a single crochet. Work loosely and continue across row, catching loops of both pieces.

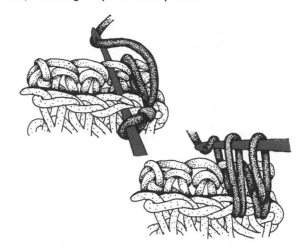

Sewing. Pin pieces with right sides together. Thread yarn needle with matching yarn and sew the pieces together loosely with an overhand stitch, catching the top loop of each stitch of both pieces.

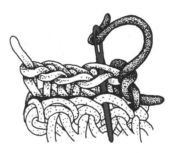

Weaving. Lay pieces face up with edges touching but not overlapping. Thread yarn needle with matching yarn and weave loosely through centers of loops of both pieces.

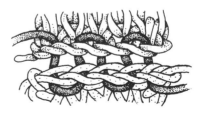

Reusing & Unkinking Yarn

Good quality yarns can be reused. Rather than discarding an out-of-style or outgrown sweater, unravel the yarn (just as you would pull out a row when you've made a mistake) and wind it into large skeins. A skein winder (swift) can be used for this job and is well worth the investment (see page 9).

Tie the skein loosely in two places with scraps of the same yarn. Dip the skein in a basin or pot of cold water until the yarn is saturated. Pull the yarn out, let it drain a bit, and then roll the skein in a terry cloth towel to blot it, as you would a sweater.

Stretch the skein over two chair backs (placed as close as necessary, back-to-back) or put it back on the skein winder and let it dry completely (if it is wool, away from direct sunlight).

If the yarn is not sufficiently unkinked, repeat the procedure.

Finishing Your Piece

Blocking or pressing will add a finishing touch to your piece. Blocking uncurls edges and evens out the definite zigs and zags where you've increased and decreased. Before the necktie (page 49) was blocked, it had very jagged edges and wouldn't lie flat. Blocking made it smooth and even.

If you've crocheted something that is almost flat, you may wish to forego formal blocking and just press it with a steam iron. On the other hand, if you have a very bulky item with lots of irregularities, it may be wise for you to send your garment out to a knit shop or a dry cleaner that specializes in blocking.

In any case, be sure to check the label on the yarn you used. It may have blocking instructions or, at the very least, laundering instructions that you can use as a guide.

If your project is made of several parts (as a sweater is, for example), block the pieces before joining them (see "Joining Two Pieces of Crochet", page 31).

Blocking

First, you have to collect your equipment.
- Ironing board or blocking board. Plywood or composition board covered with several layers of quilted material or towels and then a layer of muslin, canvas, or sheeting. All the layers must be stapled or nailed snugly to the back of the board.
- Rustproof T-pins or pushpins
- Large metal ruler or yardstick
- Basin of water or sprayer filled with water
- Heavy paper the size of your piece
- Waterproof pen or marker

Next, outline the final shape of your piece with pen or marker on the heavy paper, using a ruler to make seamlines straight and of the proper length. Tack or pin this to your blocking or ironing board.

Dip your garment in water and gently squeeze out excess water; if you prefer, spray the piece thoroughly with water.

With rustproof pins, pin the garment wrong side up to the board, following the outline on your sketch. Pin at a slant to the edge of the piece to avoid pulling the edge out of shape and making puckers. Pin at about one-inch intervals.

Allow your piece to dry thoroughly, checking occasionally to make sure the seams are straight and aren't puckering. When it's completely dry (don't rush it at this point), remove it from the board.

Pressing

Pressing calls for the same equipment as blocking; in addition, you'll need a steam iron and pressing cloth or a dry iron and an old dishtowel or cloth.

Follow the instructions for blocking, but don't wet your piece before pinning it to the board. Pin it in the same manner and then press it with the steam iron. Be sure to protect your piece (especially if it is wool) with a pressing cloth, raising and lowering the iron on the piece (don't use a back and forth motion on the cloth; instead, lift and press).

For lightly wrinkled pieces, eliminate the pressing cloth and hold the steam iron slightly above — never on — the garment.

If you use a dry iron, wet a dishtowel or cloth, wring it out, and lay it on the piece. Press with the iron (again, use a lift and press motion; don't go back and forth), rewetting the towel as necessary until the whole piece is pressed.

Leave the piece on the board until completely dry.

Crocheting Geometric Shapes

When you begin experimenting with your own designs, you can have some fun working with basic shapes and forms. Visualize your idea as a combination of tubes, triangles, ovals, and circles, and you'll

Bizarre "Self Portrait to Wear" is an advanced construction based on a combination of a variety of geometric shapes. Design: Lynne Streeter.

be able to create anything without a pattern. If you analyze the crocheted dog and body shown below, you'll see that they are merely combinations of shapes.

When crocheting geometric shapes, use a slip stitch at the end of each round to taper the stitches down to the level of the last round and to join one round to the next.

Circle. Begin by making a ring (see page 14 or 22). For the first round (each time around is called a round), work a stitch into each stitch of the ring. Work the next round into stitches of the first round. Continue working each round into the stitches of the previous round, increasing where necessary to prevent any puckering.

When crocheting in the round, you will need to mark the end of each round with a scrap of bright yarn. The piece will look like a spiral; without a marker, it's hard to tell where one row ends and the next row begins.

Square. Begin with a ring, then make 1 round of stitches. For the second round, work 1 stitch in each stitch, except at the corners, where you'll work 3 stitches in each stitch. On the third and all succeeding rounds, work 1 stitch in each stitch, except at corners, where you work 1 stitch in the first stitch, 3 stitches in the middle stitch, and 1 stitch in the third stitch.

Hexagon and octagon. Work the same as for the square but put in 6 or 8 corners instead of 4. To make corners, put 3 stitches in one.

Oval. Start with a chain of at least 5 stitches. For the first round, work on both sides of the foundation chain, putting 1 stitch in each chain, except at the beginning and end of the chain, where you put 3 stitches to round the corners. Continue around, putting 1 stitch in each stitch on the sides of the oval and increasing as necessary in the ends to round the edges and keep the piece flat.

Triangle and diamond. Start with 2 chains, insert the hook in the first chain, and make 1 single crochet. Turn, make 3 single crochets in the 1 single crochet you have just made, chain 1, turn. Begin to increase in this row: put 2 single crochets in the first stitch, 1 single crochet in the second, 2 single crochets in the third. Continue in this manner, increasing in the first and last stitch of each row. To form a diamond, decrease on the second half of the piece in the same manner as you increased.

Tube (cylinder) and bowl. Begin with a ring; then make 1 stitch in each stitch of the ring. Continue to make a long spiral without increasing or decreasing until tube is desired length. For a bowl, increase after the first few rounds; then work 1 stitch in each stitch for a few rounds; then decrease evenly over the next rows until top is desired diameter.

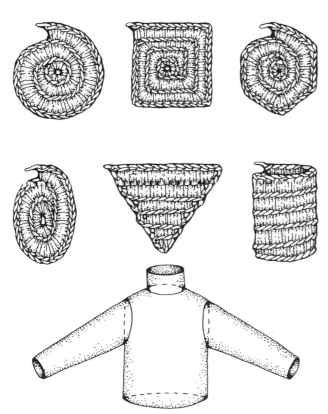

Simple geometric shapes, *the basis for any construction, include (upper left and reading clockwise) circle, square, hexagon, oval, triangle, tube. Pullover sweater made of four tubes illustrates this point.*

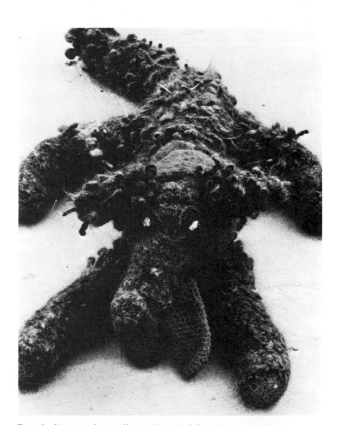

Break down *a three-dimensional object into geometric shapes and you'll be able to combine tubes, triangles, and circles into anything you wish to make — including this lovable canine friend. Design: Mary Moser.*

Breeze through summer *in a cool sundress with a crocheted linen bodice and fabric skirt in complementary colors.*
Design: Karen Cummings.
Halter Dress: Instructions on facing page.

Chains and half-double crochet *create the floral motifs in this easy-to-make halter top.*
Design: H. Louyse Younger and Karen Cummings.
Halter top: Instructions on facing page.

A Potpourri of Projects

you can make

From a simple halter top to a made-for-lazing hammock, the projects on the following 35 pages are designed for crocheters with varying degrees of experience. Quickly scanning the instructions given with each project will tell you if the project suits your experience as a crocheter.

The sizes given for clothing are meant only as guides; they cannot be considered as absolutes since fit is dependent on current styles, as well as on how tight or loose you like your clothing. Blocking of woolen garments should correct slight variations in size (see page 32).

Before you begin to crochet any of the projects, *be sure to make a test swatch* to check your stitch gauge; otherwise your garment will not fit when completed. Changing hook size will help you to get the correct stitch gauge. Remember that a test swatch is especially important when you're working with hand spun yarns of unconventional plies and sizes. See pages 29-30 for more information on stitch gauge.

Halter Tops

(Color photos on facing page)

These are fairly simple beginner projects which involve increasing. The halter dress and halter top are based on the same pattern, but the top has a floral motif worked in the middle. It can be made empire style, as shown, or waist-length like the one attached to the skirt.

Halter Top

Materials: 2 ounces 4-ply knitting worsted
G aluminum crochet hook (or hook to give proper gauge)
Gauge: 4 stitches = 1 inch; 3 rows = 1 inch
Main Stitch: Half double crochet
Size: 8-12

Ch 29.

Rows 1-4: Work same as for halter dress (see right).

Row 5: 2 hdc in top of 2nd st (inc made), hdc in next 8 sts, ch 4, * sk 1st st, dc in next st, rep from * 3x, ch 4, sk 1 st, hdc across to last 2 sts, 2 hdc in next st (inc made), hdc in turning ch, ch 2, turn.

Row 6: 2 hdc in 2nd st, hdc in next 9 sts, ch 4, sc in top of each dc (4 sc), ch 4, hdc across to last 2 sts, 2 hdc in next st, hdc in turning ch, ch 2, turn.

Row 7: 2 hdc in 2nd st, hdc in next 10 sts, ch 4, sc in each sc, ch 4, hdc to last 2 sts, 2 hdc in next st, hdc in turning ch, ch 2, turn.

Row 8: 2 hdc in 2nd st, hdc in next 11 sts, ch 4, sc in each sc, ch 4, hdc to last 2 sts, 2 hdc in next st, hdc in turning ch, ch 2, turn.

Row 9: 2 hdc in 2nd st, hdc in next 12 sts, * ch 1, dc in sc, rep from * 3x, ch 1, hdc across to last 2 sts, 2 hdc in next st, hdc in turning ch, ch 2, turn.

Row 10: 2 hdc in 2nd st, hdc across row (at pattern, hdc in each ch and dc of previous row).

Rows 11-13: Work same as for halter dress (43 hdc).

Row 14: 2 hdc in top of 2nd st, hdc in next 15 sts, ch 4, * sk 1st st, dc in next st, rep from * 3x, ch 4, sk 1 st, hdc across to last 2 sts, 2 hdc in next st, hdc in turning ch, ch 2, turn.

Row 15: Hdc in 2nd st and in next 16 sts, ch 4, sc in top of next 4 dc, ch 4, hdc across row and in turning ch, ch 2, turn.

Row 16: 2 hdc in top of 2nd st, hdc in next 16 sts, ch 4, sc in next 4 sc, ch 4, hdc across to last 2 sts, 2 hdc in next st, hdc in turning ch, ch 2, turn.

Row 17: 2 hdc in top of 2nd st, hdc in next 17 sts, ch 4, sc in next 4 sc, ch 4, hdc across to last 2 sts, 2 hdc in next st, hdc in turning ch, ch 2, turn.

Row 18: 2 hdc in top of 2nd st, hdc in next 18 sts, * ch 1, dc in next sc, rep from * 3x, ch 1, hdc across to last 2 sts, 2 hdc in next st, hdc in turning ch, ch 2, turn.

Row 19: 2 hdc in top of 2nd st, hdc across (at pattern, hdc in each ch and dc of previous row) to last 2 sts, 2 hdc in next st, hdc in turning ch (53 hdc), ch 2, turn.

Rows 20-26: Hdc across each row, inc'ing at each end.

To Make Ties: Working in same direction, ch 40, turn. Sc in 1st ch from hook and in each ch until corner is reached (bottom tie made); work along side, making 1 sc in end of each row; at top corner, ch 40, turn, sc in 1st ch and in each ch (neck tie made); sc across top, ch 40, making 2nd neck tie as before; sc down side, making 1 sc in end of each row, ch 40, turn; make bottom tie as before, making 1 sc in each st along bottom; join with sl st, end off.

Halter Dress

Materials: One tube of 3-ply linen yarn (sold on 1 pound tubes, one tube will make several halters) *or* 5 ounces of 4-ply knitting worsted.
G aluminum crochet hook (or hook to give proper gauge)
Fourteen ½-inch beads
Wrap-around or gathered skirt
Gauge: 4 stitches = 1 inch; 5 rows = 2 inches
Main Stitch: Half double crochet
Size: 8-12

Ch 29.

Row 1: Hdc in 3rd ch from hook and into each ch across (28 hdc), ch 2, turn.

Row 2: Sk 1st st, hdc in 2nd st and in each st of previous row, ch 2, turn.

Row 3: 2 hdc in top of 2nd st (inc made), hdc across row to last 2 sts, 2 hdc in next st (inc made), hdc in top of turning ch, ch 2, turn (30 hdc).

Row 4: Rep row 2.

Rows 5-10: Rep row 3, inc'ing 1 st each end (42 hdc).

Row 11: Hdc across row and in turning ch (42 hdc).

Row 12: Hdc across row, inc'ing at each end (44 hdc).

Row 13: Rep row 11 (44 hdc).

Row 14: Rep row 12 (46 hdc).

Row 15: Rep row 11 (46 hdc).

Rows 16-27: Rep row 12 (70 hdc).

Rows 28-31: Rep row 11. (If using knitting worsted, rep row 11 five more times, or until proper length.)

Row 32: Hdc across row, 2 hdc and 1 sc in top of turning ch. Do not turn, but working along side of halter, sc in end of each row. When last side st reached, ch 30 or desired length for tie, turn, sc in 1st ch from hook and in each ch until corner is reached (tie made). Sc across top of halter, ch 30, turn, sc in 1st ch from hook and in each ch until corner reached (tie made). Work down last side, sc in end of each row. End off.

To Finish: Sew halter top to a purchased or home sewn wrap-around or gathered skirt. Slip two beads over the end of each tie at neck and secure with an overhand knot. Thread remaining beads for front of halter top with linen yarn and tie or sew to neckline.

Garden Cardigan

This V-neck cardigan not only keeps you warm — its basic style fits in anywhere. Since the plain V-neck vest on page 43 is essentially the same style, cardigan and vest could be worn as a set.

Materials: 4-ounce skeins of off-white 4-ply acrylic knitting worsted (small, 5 skeins; medium and large, 6 skeins)
H aluminum crochet hook (or hook to give proper gauge)
Buttons
Gauge: 4 stitches = 1 inch; 5 rows = 1 inch; Ribbing: 4 sc = 1 inch
Main Stitch: Single crochet
Size: Directions are for small (32-34). Changes for medium (36-38) and large (40-42) are in parentheses.

Back and Front

Ch 13 to measure 3 inches.

Row 1 (Ribbing): Sc in 2nd ch from hook and in each ch across (12 sc), ch 1, turn.

Row 2 (Ribbing): Sc in back lp of 1st sc and in back lp of each sc across. Rep row 2 for 132(146,160) rows. Ch 1, turn.

Row 3: Work 132(146,160) sc along long edge of ribbing, ch 1, turn.

Row 4: Work sc in 1st sc and in each sc across row. Rep row 2 until piece measures 15½(16,16¾) inches from bottom of rib or to desired length to underarm.

Dec 1 sc at neck edge by working 2 sc together, work 28(31,34) sc, ch 1, turn.

Shape Armhole and Neck: Dec 1 sc at armhole edge every row (6,7,9)x. At the same time, dec 1 sc at neck edge every other row 8(10,10)x. Work until armhole measures 7¼(7¾,8¼) inches, end at armhole edge. Sl st across 7(8,8) sc. Work to neck edge, ch 1, turn. Work 8(8,8) sc. End off.

Back Armhole: Sk 6(8,8) sc, attach yarn, work 60(64,72) sc, ch 1, turn. Dec 1 sc each side every row 6(7,9)x. Work for 7¼(7¾,8¼) inches, sl st across 7(8,8) sc. Work 34(36,38) sc, ch 1, turn. Sl st across 8(8,8) sts. Work 18(20,22) sc. End off.

Shape Armhole and Neck: Sk 6(8,8) sc, attach yarn, work across 31st row, dec 1 sc at neck edge. Dec 1 sc at armhole edge every row 6(7,9)x. At the same time, dec 1 sc at neck edge every other row 8(10,10)x. Work until armhole measures 7¼(7¾,8¼) inches. End at armhole edge. Sl st across 7(8,8) sc. Work to neck edge, ch 1, turn. Work 8(8,8) sc. End off. Join shoulders by overcasting.

Sleeves (make 2)

Ch 13 to measure 3 inches. Work ribbing same as for

Washable acrylic yarn *makes white cardigan practical for gardening chores. Design: Katherine Dauth.*

body for 35(38,40) rows, ch 1, turn. Work (tightly) 35(38,40) sc along long edge of ribbing, ch 1, turn. Work sc in 1st sc and in each sc across, ch 1, turn. Checking gauge periodically, rep last row, inc'ing 1 st each end every 7(8,8) rows 9(9,9)x. Work until piece measures 17½(18¼,19) inches from bottom of rib.

Sleeve Cap: Sl st across 3(4,4) sc, work 47(48,50) sc, ch 1, turn. Dec 1 sc each end every other row 2(5,6)x. Dec 1 sc each end every row 16(13,13)x. End off; 11(12,12) sc remain.

To Finish: Join sleeves to sweater by overcasting. Attach yarn at lower front edge and work 87(91,95) sc along front edge, 18(20,22) sc along back of neck, 87(91,95) sc along opposite front edge, ch 1, turn. Work a total of 5 rows of sc along front and back neck edges. If buttonholes are desired, on row 3 work sc to where you would like a buttonhole, * ch 3, sk 3 sc, continue to work 1 sc in every sc until next place for buttonhole, rep from *. On row 4, work 1 sc in every sc and 3 sc in the ch-3 sp. Sew on buttons.

Granny's Vests

You can use leftover yarn scraps (granny squares are crochet's answer to the traditional patchwork quilt) or buy one small skein of each color as indicated below to make these colorful granny vests.

To change sizes, follow the diagrams below or adjust further by eliminating squares where necessary.

Materials: One 2-ounce skein sport weight yarn in *each* of 7 colors — red, turquoise, purple, yellow, green, orange, pink (or use leftover yarns)
F aluminum crochet hook (or hook to give proper gauge)
Yarn needle

Gauge: Square #1 = 3 inches; #2 = 4 inches; #3 = 5 inches; #4 = 12 inches

Main Stitch: Double crochet

Size: Small (child's): six #1 squares, eight #2 squares, one #4 square. Medium and large (woman's): six #2 squares and fourteen #3 squares. See diagrams at right for placement of squares.

Note: Each time you complete one square of stitches on a granny square, you have completed what will be referred to as one row. Since each row measures one inch in height, you will add one row to the basic 3-inch square (square #1) to get the 4-inch square (square #2), and so on. The 12-inch square (square #4) will be a total of 12 rows.

For every square, change colors after each row.

To make the basic 3-inch square:

Row 1: With color A, ch 3 and form a ring by making a sl st in 1st ch. Ch 3, 2 dc in ring; ch 2, 3 dc in ring; ch 2, 3 dc in ring; ch 2, 3 dc in ring; ch 2, join with sl st in top of ch-3. Tie off color A (draw yarn through final lp and cut yarn).

Row 2: With color B, make a slip knot around ch-2 sp of previous row. Continue by making a ch 2, then 2 dc, ch 2, 3 dc (all in the same sp), ch 2. * 3 dc, ch 2, 3 dc in next sp, ch 2, rep from * in the next 2 sps. Join with a sl st to top of ch 2. End off.

Row 3: Change colors at the beginning of each row. Beginning in a corner with a slip knot, ch 2, 2 dc, ch 2, 3 dc, ch 2; in next sp (side of square), * 3 dc, ch 2, 3 dc, ch 2, 3 dc, ch 2. Rep from * 2x. Ch 2. End off.

For following rows (add one row for square #2, 2 rows for square #3, 9 rows for square #4): Always begin with a slip knot, ch 2, 2 dc, ch 2, 3 dc, ch 2 in 1st corner. For sides, work 3 dc and ch 2; for all other corners, work 3 dc, ch 2, 3 dc, ch 2. End with a sl st.

To Assemble Vests: First, weave in loose ends with yarn needle. Then, following diagram for correct size, join squares with color of your choice and hook, using a sl st, or sew together, using yarn needle. When

Mother and daughter *can use yarn leftovers to crochet their matching granny vests. Design: Francoise Kirkman.*

Placement of squares for vests

small

	4	
1		1
1		1
1		1

2	2	2	2
2	2	2	2

3	3
3	3
3	3
2	2
2	2
2	2

3	3	3	3
3	3	3	3

medium & large

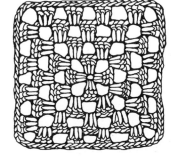

A four-inch square *should look like this. Each row of squares measures one inch.*

all squares are assembled, use contrasting color and same hook and sc in each stitch around edges of vest. Add ch 1 at corners if necessary to prevent puckering.

To Make Ties: Using color of your choice and F hook, ch 176, turn and sl st into each ch. At end of row, ch 2 and sl st into sts of previous row. End off. Weave into spaces in fronts of vest.

Beach Bikini

Sun-lovers will want to crochet this comfortable bikini made of acrylic worsted weight yarn. The lightweight yarn dries quickly and will not stretch when wet.

Materials: 4-ply acrylic knitting worsted: one 4-ounce skein color A (rose), one 2-ounce skein color B (wine), one 2-ounce skein color C (blue)
H aluminum crochet hook (or hook to give proper gauge)
Yarn needle
Narrow swimwear elastic
Gauge: 4 stitches = 1 inch; 3 rows = 1 inch
Main Stitch: Half double crochet
Size: 5-9

Top

With color A and beginning at top, loosely ch 6.
Row 1: Hdc in 4th ch from hook, ch 1, 2 hdc in last ch, turn.
Row 2: Ch 3 (counts as 1st hdc), hdc in 1st hdc, hdc in next hdc, (hdc, ch 1, hdc) in ch-1 sp, hdc in next hdc, hdc in top of ch-3 (you have 7 hdc), turn.
Row 3: Ch 3, hdc in 1st hdc, hdc in each hdc across row, working (hdc, ch 1, hdc) in center ch-1 sp (you have 10 hdc), turn.
Rows 4-8: Rep row 3 (25 hdc).
Row 9: Ch 3, hdc in each hdc across row, making 1 hdc in each ch-1 sp (you have 26 hdc), turn.
Row 10: Ch 3, hdc in each st across row. At end of row, 2 hdc in top of ch-3 (you have 27 hdc), turn.
Row 11: Rep row 10 (you have 28 hdc). End off. Rep rows 1-11 for 2nd cup.
Note: For larger size, rep row 10 as necessary for fit. Join cups at center bottom edge with sl st.

Trim: *Center motif:* With color B, on right side at bottom edge, join yarn in 4th st from center. Working toward center, ch 2, hdc in next st, dc in next st, tr in next st, skipping place where color was joined. Tr in next st, dc in next st, hdc in next st, sc and end off in next st.

Top motif on cups: On right side with color B, join yarn in top of turning ch of 1st row. Working toward center, ch 2, yo, insert hook into next st, yo, draw through, yo, draw through 2 lps on hook (2 lps on hook), yo 2x, insert hook into center st, yo, draw through lp, yo, draw through 2 lps on hook 2x (3 lps on hook), yo, insert hook into next st, yo, draw through 1 lp, yo, draw through 2 lps on hook (4 lps on hook), insert hook into next st, yo, draw through, yo, draw through 1 lp on hook, yo, draw through 5 lps on hook. End off. Rep on other cup.

To Give Body and Stretch: Measure length along bottom edge of cups and cut a piece of narrow swimwear elastic about 1 to 1½ inches shorter than the necessary length. Attach elastic with needle and thread at both outer corner stitches at bottom edge. Encase in edge trim.

Edging: With right side facing you, bottom edge up, join color C at right corner of bottom edge. Working around elastic, sc into each st along bottom edge, sc into same sp where center motif joins and into top of each st across motif. Sc in same sp as motif ends and in each st across to corner, 3 sc in corner. Working along outer side of left cup, sc in end of each row and into each ch-2 of motif, 3 sc in top of motif to turn. Working along inner edge of left cup, sc into side of motif and end of each row to center. In last st at center, insert hook, draw yarn through (2 lps on hook). Working along inner edge of right cup, in end of 1st row at bottom, insert hook, draw yarn through, yo, draw yarn through 3 lps on hook. Continue around edge in same manner, joining with sl st, ch 2, and continue working around on right side, making a sc in between each sc of previous row. Working around elastic, work to last sp on bottom edge.

To Make Ties: Ch 63, turn (being careful not to twist chain), sc in 3rd ch from hook and into each ch back to corner. In last ch, insert hook, yo and draw through a lp (2 lps on hook). Working along outer side of left cup, insert hook in between 1st sp between sts at corner, yo, draw through a lp (3 lps on hook), insert hook into next sp, yo, draw through a lp, yo, draw through 4 lps on hook. Continue along side, making a sc into each sp between sc of previous rows. When corner is reached, make tie as before. Continue working around outer edge in same manner. Join with sl st. End off.

Bottom (front)

With color A, ch 9.
Row 1: Hdc in 3rd ch from hook and in each ch across, ch 2, turn (turning ch counts as 1st hdc of next row throughout pattern).
Rows 2-3: Hdc across row, ch 2, turn.
Row 4: 2 hdc in 1st st (inc made), hdc across row to last st, 2 hdc in last st (inc made), ch 2, turn (10 hdc).
Row 5: Hdc across row, ch 2, turn.
Rows 6-14: Rep row 4, inc'ing at each end (at end of row 14, you will have 28 hdc).
Row 15: 2 hdc in 1st st, hdc across row to last st, 2 hdc in last st, ch 5, turn (30 hdc).
Row 16: Hdc in 3rd ch from hook and in next 2 chs, hdc in top of each st across row, 2 hdc in last st, ch 5, turn (34 hdc).
Rows 17-19: Rep row 16 (46 hdc).
Row 20: Hdc in each st, ch 2, turn.
Row 21: 2 hdc in 1st st, hdc across row to last st, 2 hdc in last st, ch 2, turn.
Row 22: Hdc across row, ch 2, turn.
Row 23: Rep row 21 (50 hdc).
Rows 24-25: Hdc across rows. End off.

Bottom (back)

Ch 9.
Row 1: Hdc in 3rd ch from hook and in each ch across (8 hdc), ch 2, turn.

Bikini of washable yarn *has surprise color accents on the top and on the waistline. Design: Karen Cummings.*

. . . *Bikini (cont'd.)*

Rows 2-18: 2 hdc in 1st st (inc made), hdc across row to last st, 2 hdc in last st (inc made), ch 2, turn (42 hdc).

Row 19: 2 hdc in 1st st, hdc across row to last st, 2 hdc in last st, ch 5, turn (44 hdc).

Row 20: Hdc in 3rd ch from hook and in next 2 chs, hdc in top of each st across row, 2 hdc in last st, ch 5, turn (48 hdc).

Row 21: Rep row 20 (52 hdc).

Rows 22-25: Hdc across rows. End off. Sew sides and crotch together or sl st together.

Trim: *Legs:* **Row 1:** Join color C to leg opening at side seam. Ch 2, sc in ends of rows around leg (1 sc in each row), holding elastic to back side of bikini and encasing it in each sc st as for top. **Row 2:** Sc in each sc of previous row. End off.

Front Motif: **Row 1:** Holding front right side facing you, in top edge join color B in top of 22nd hdc, ch 2. Holding elastic to back, hdc around elastic in next st, continuing to keep elastic to back side and encased in sts, dc in next st, tr in next 2 sts, dc in next st, sc in next st. End off. Join color C in next st, ch 2, sc in each st around top (keep elastic encased), sc across top of motif. **Row 2:** Sc in between sc of 1st row and around elastic, sc across top of motif. End off.

Try on suit; pull elastic on legs and around top to fit snugly. Then tie elastic to itself and thread ends into sts to conceal.

Hooded Cape & Lacy Shawl

(Color photos on page 42)

Summer holidays in Spain and chilly autumn days in Ireland seem to be the occasions for the two cover-ups shown on page 42.

The cape would be a challenge for an intermediate crocheter, not because of its complexity but because of its bulk. Although it takes quite a bit of yarn and quite a few hours of work, the final result is well worth the effort.

A simpler project, our shawl for Spanish evenings is composed of squares and half-squares in a lacy floral pattern. Because the half-square is somewhat complicated, you should tackle and master the whole square first.

Cape

Chase the fog and cold away with a classic cape made of concise single crochet. The hood and cape-let section, attached to the cape with tiny buttons, can be removed to show the stand-up mandarin style collar underneath. Since the cape is worked from the neck down, you can make it the length that suits you the best.

Materials: 2½ pounds lightweight Donegal Tweed for the cape; 1½ pounds for the capelet and hood
H and J aluminum crochet hooks (or hooks to give proper gauge)
Buttons
Gauge: 7 stitches = 2 inches; 7 rows = 2 inches (for J hook)
Main Stitch: Single crochet
Size: One size fits all

Cape

Using H hook, ch 54.

Row 1: 1 sc in 2nd ch from hook and in each of next 52 chs (53 sc), ch 1, turn.

Row 2: 1 sc in each sc, ch 1, turn.

Row 3: Change to J hook. Begin pat row. * 1 sc in next 5 sc, 2 sc in next sc. Rep from * 7x. 1 sc in next 4 sc, 2 sc in last sc, ch 1, turn. (Note: Each time you do a pat row, you inc by one the number of single scs worked. For example, row 3: **5** sc and **4** sc; row 4: **6** sc and **5** sc; and so forth.)

Row 4: * 1 sc in next 6 sc, 2 sc in next sc. Rep from * 7x. 1 sc in next 5 sc, 2 sc in last sc, ch 1, turn.

(Continued on next page)

Rows 5-7: 1 sc in each sc, ch 1, turn.

Rows 8-9: Work 2 pat rows. Remember to ch 1, turn at end of **each** row.

Rows 10-12: 1 sc in each sc, ch 1, turn (89 sts).

Rows 13-14: Work pattern rows (107 sts).

Rows 15-17: 1 sc in each sc, ch 1, turn (107 sts).

Rows 18-19: Work pattern rows (125 sts).

Rows 20-22: 1 sc in each sc, ch 1, turn.

Row 23: *Shape shoulder.* 1 sc in 1st 28 sc, dec 1 sc, * 1 sc in next 4 sc, dec 1 sc, rep from * 1x. 1 sc in next 59 sc, dec 1 sc, 1 sc in next 4 sc, dec 1 sc, 1 sc in next 4 sc, dec 1 sc, sc to end, ch 1, turn (119 sts).

Row 24: 1 sc in next 27 sc, dec 1 sc, * 1 sc in next 4 sc, dec 1 sc, rep from * 1x. 1 sc in next 55 sc, dec 1 sc, 1 sc in next 4 sc, dec 1 sc, 1 sc in next 4 sc, dec 1 sc, sc to end, ch 1, turn (113 sts).

Row 25: 1 sc in next 50 sc, * 2 sc in next sc, 1 sc in next 3 sc, rep from * 2x, sc to end (116 sts).

Rows 26-27: Work pat rows. Rep the last pat row combination for row 27 (13 and 12). You have 134 sts.

Rows 28-30: 1 sc in each sc, ch 1, turn.

Rows 31-32: Work pat rows (152 sts).

Rows 33-35: 1 sc in each sc, ch 1, turn.

Rows 36-37: Work pat rows (170 sts).

Rows 38-40: 1 sc in each sc, ch 1, turn.

Rows 41-42: Work pat rows (188 sts).

Rows 43-45: 1 sc in each sc, ch 1, turn.

Rows 46-47: Work pat rows (206 sts).

Rows 48-50: 1 sc in each sc, ch 1, turn.

Rows 51-52: Work pat rows (224 sts).

Rows 53-55: 1 sc in each sc.

Rows 56-80: Begin to form arm slits, which are worked in three parts (see illustration below).

Arm slits are made by crocheting three extensions; these will be joined later.

Part 1: Continuing in the same manner as for sc rows. * 1 sc in next 32 sc, ch 1, turn. Rep from * and work 24 more rows. Cut yarn and secure end.

Part 2: Attach yarn to st exactly next to st where you ended part 1 of row 55. * 1 sc in next 160 sc, ch 1, turn. Rep from * and work 24 more rows. Cut yarn and secure end.

Part 3: Attach yarn to st exactly next to the st where you ended part 2 of row 55. * 1 sc in next 32 sc, ch 1, turn. Rep from * and work 24 more rows.

To Finish: Sc along the next row, joining arm slits as you come to them. Ch 1, turn, and do a 2nd row of sc. Work remainder of cape in this manner until cape is about 2 inches shorter than you desire. (With wear, the cape will get a little longer.) End off.

Buttonholes: (To make the buttonhole panel stronger, put hook directly in center of st instead of picking up two loops on sc st.)

Attach yarn to right-hand neck edge.

Row 1: (Put 1 sc down to match each row across.) 1 sc in each st, ch 1, turn.

Row 2: 1 sc in each sc, working up to right neck edge where you began, ch 1, turn.

Row 3: 1 sc in next 3 sc, * ch 2, sk next 2 sc, 1 sc in next 8 sc. Rep from * 10 *more* times for 12 buttonholes. 1 sc in each st to bottom, ch 1, turn.

Row 4: 1 sc in each sc. When you reach a ch sp, put 2 sc in this sp. Work to top neck edge, ch 1, turn.

Row 5: 1 sc in each sc, ch 1, turn.

Row 6: 1 sc in each sc. When you come to neck edge, sc all around neck and down the left side of cape, again putting 1 sc down to match each row across. Then, sc up left side, ending at neck edge. End off.

Collar: Attach yarn to right-hand neck edge.

Row 1: 1 sc in next 5 sc, * ch 1, sk 1 sc, 1 sc in next 10 sc. Rep from * 3x. Sc in next 5 sc, ch 1, turn. You will not quite reach the end of the neck edge. (The left and right collars will not overlap but will meet at center front.) The holes formed by the ch-1 sp are buttonholes that correspond to buttons you will sew on the capelet.

Row 2: 1 sc in each sc and ch-1 sp, ch 1, turn.

Rows 3-6: 1 sc in each sc to end, ch 1, turn.

Row 7: 1 sc in each sc. End off.

Capelet

Using H hook, ch 54.

Row 1: 1 sc in 2nd ch from hook and in next 52 chs (53 sc), ch 1, turn.

Row 2: Pat row: * 1 sc in next 5 sc, 2 sc in next sc. Rep from * 7x. 1 sc in next 4 sc, 2 sc in last sc, ch 1, turn.

Row 3: * 1 sc in next 6 sc, 2 sc in next sc. Rep from * 7x. 1 sc in next 5 sc, 2 sc in last sc, ch 1, turn. (Note: Work pat rows as in cape, inc'ing in each pat row the number of scs by one.)

Rows 4-6: Change to J hook and work pat rows. Ch 1, turn at end of each row.

Rows 7-11: 1 sc in each sc to end. Ch 1, turn at end of each row.

Rows 12-14: Work pat rows, ch 1, turn at end of each row.

Rows 15-19: 1 sc in each sc to end. Ch 1, turn at end of each row. Continue working pat rows and 5 sc rows until capelet is desired length (about to the elbow). End off.

Hood (Make 2)

Using J hook, ch 29.

Row 1: 1 sc in 2nd ch from hook and in each ch to end, ch 1, turn.

Rows 2-47: 1 sc in each sc, ch 1, turn.

Row 48: 1 sc in each sc until 5 sts from end, dec 1 sc, 1 sc in last 3 sc, ch 1, turn.

Row 49: 1 sc in each sc, ch 1, turn.

Row 50: Rep row 48.

Row 51: Rep row 49.

Row 52: Rep row 48.

Row 53: Rep row 49.

Row 54: 1 sc in next 16 sc, dec 1 sc, sc in next 2 sc, dec 1 sc, sc in each sc to end, ch 1, turn.

Row 55: 1 sc in each sc, ch 1, turn.

Row 56: 1 sc in next 14 sc, * dec 1 sc, sc in next 2 sc, dec 1 sc, sc to end, ch 1, turn.

Row 57: 1 sc in each sc, ch 1, turn.

Row 58: 1 sc in next 12 sc. Rep pat (* to end) of row 56.

Row 59: 1 sc in each sc, ch 1, turn.

Row 60: 1 sc in next 10 sc, rep pat (* to end) of row 56.

Row 61: 1 sc in each sc, ch 1, turn.

Row 62: 1 sc in next 8 sc. Rep pat (* to end) of row 56.

Row 63: 1 sc in each sc, ch 1, turn.

Row 64: 1 sc in next 6 sc. Rep pat (* to end) of row 56.

Row 65: 1 sc in each sc, ch 1, turn.

Row 66: 1 sc in each sc until 2 sts from end, dec 1 sc. You should have two pieces that look like this.

With sc, attach the two pieces along the back of hood (indicated by broken lines). Next, make 3 rows of sc around the part that frames the face (indicated by dots). End off.

To Finish: With sc, attach neck edge of hood (indicated by xs) to neck edge of capelet. Block cape and capelet. When blocking be careful to even out fullness in the cape and capelet and to shape the shoulders of both. Sew tiny buttons on inside neck edge of capelet to correspond to buttonholes on cape neck edge. Sew buttons down front of cape.

Shawl

A perfect complement to any wardrobe, our quick-to-crochet shawl is a series of 4-inch granny squares. The decorative motifs are the floral square and the floral half-square shown at right.

Materials: 12 ounces turquoise sport weight yarn. G aluminum crochet hook (or hook to give proper gauge)
Yarn needle
Gauge: 1 square = 4 inches
Main Stitch: Double crochet

Motif (Make 49)
Ch 10. Join with a sl st to form a ring.

Rnd 1: Ch 2, 4 dc in ring, (ch 9, 5 dc in ring)3x, ch 9. Join with sl st to top of ch-2.

Rnd 2: Ch 2, 1 dc in each of next 2 dc, * ch 2, 1 dc in same dc with last dc, 1 dc in each of next 2 dc, ch 2; under next ch-9, work 3 dc, ch 5, 3 dc for corner; ch 2, 1 dc in each of next 3 dc, rep from * around, ending ch 2, sl st in top of 1st ch-2.

Rnd 3: Ch 2, (yo, draw up lp in next dc, yo and draw yarn through 2 lps)5x, yo and draw yarn through 6

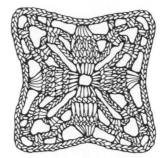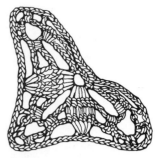

Whole and half *floral motifs for shawl should look like these. You'll need 49 full and 12 half motifs.*

lps, * ch 5, sk 1 dc, 1 dc in middle dc, ch 3; under next ch work 2 dc, ch 2, 2 dc; ch 3, sk 1 dc, 1 dc in next dc, ch 5, (yo, draw up lp in next dc, yo and draw yarn through 2 lps)6x (6 hdc), yo and draw yarn through 7 lps, rep from * around, ending ch 5, sk 1 dc, 1 dc in next dc, ch 3; under next ch-5, work 2 dc, ch 2, 2 dc; ch 3, sk 1 dc, 1 dc in next dc, ch 5, join with sl st to top of 1st cluster.

Rnd 4: 1 sc in each ch and in back lp of each dc, working 2 dc under ch-2 at each corner. Join with sl st and end off.

Half Motif (Make 12)
Ch 10. Join with sl st to form a ring.

Rnd 1: Ch 11, 5 dc in ring, ch 9, 5 dc in ring, ch 11, sl st in ring.

Rnd 2: Ch 2, turn work. (3 dc, ch 5, 3 dc) in ch-11 lp, * ch 2, 1 dc in each of 3 dc, ch 2, 1 dc in same dc with last dc, 1 dc in each of next 2 dc, ch 2; (3 dc, ch 5, 3 dc) under next ch-11 lp, rep from *, ch 2, join with sl st in round circle.

Rnd 3: Ch 5, turn work. * 1 dc in middle dc, ch 3; under next ch, work 2 dc, ch 2, 2 dc; ch 3, 1 dc in middle dc, ch 5, (yo, draw up lp in next dc, yo and through 2 lps)6x, yo and through all 7 lps, ch 5, rep from *, end with 1 dc in middle dc, ch 5 and join at original circle.

Rnd 4: 1 sc in each ch and in back lp of each dc, working 2 dc under ch-2 at each corner. Join and end off.

To Finish: Following diagram below, lay out motifs and half motifs. With right sides up, sc or sew edges of each motif together from corner dc to 7th sc along edge. End off, leaving 10 sc free to form diamond shape with motif next to it. Edge shawl with sc or dc.

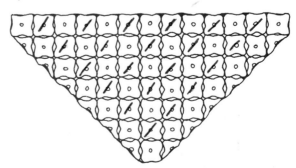

Placement of squares and half squares for shawl

Wear this lacy shawl *to castles in Spain or to a barbecue in your back yard. Design: Joice M. Beatty.*
Shawl: Instructions begin on page 41.

Making this cape *is an ambitious project, but it's worth the effort; its classic style will endure the whims of fashion. Design: Laurel Keeley.*
Cape: Instructions begin on page 39.

Crochet a simple vest *or decorate it with a tranquil scene by following the color chart. Designs: Plain vest, Katherine Dauth; scenic vest, Kathy McBride.*
Plain and Scenic Vests: Instructions on facing page.

Variations on a Vest - Plain & Fancy

(Color photos on facing page)

The off-white vest and scenic vest with hills, clouds, and a sun are both made from the same simple, classic pattern. You create the unusual effect of the scenic vest by carrying along several colors of yarn in each row of the pattern. Then, as each is needed, you pick it up (as you would pick up a new strand of yarn) and use it to make the design. For more information on this technique, see "Color Through Color," pages 30 to 31.

Both vests were designed to be worn with the V-necked cardigan shown on page 36.

Materials: Solid color vest: three 4-ounce skeins of off-white knitting worsted; scenic vest: one 4-ounce skein *each* brown, green, white, blue, and one 2-ounce skein of yellow

H aluminum crochet hook (or hook to give proper gauge)

Gauge: 11 stitches = 3 inches; 14 rows = 3 inches

Main Stitch: Single crochet

Size: Small (30-32). Changes for medium (34) and large (36) are in parentheses.

Back

Ribbing: Ch 12. **Row 1:** Sc in 2nd ch from hook and in each ch across (11 sts = 3 inches). **Row 2:** Sc in back lp of each sc, ch 1, turn. Rep row 2 until piece measures 14½ (16½ ,18¼) inches, ch 1, turn. Work sc in top of 1st row of ribbing, then work 53(59,65) sc along long edge of ribbing, ch 1, turn. Continue working rows of sc, inc'ing 1 st *each* end every 2 inches 3(4,5)x until entire piece measures 11(11½,12) inches, ch 1, turn.

Shape Armhole: Sl st across 3(5,6) sc, work to within 3(5,6) sc, ch 1, turn. Dec 1 sc at each armhole edge every other row 4(5,6)x, ch 1, turn. Continue working until armhole measures 7½ (8,8½) inches. Sl st across 3(3,4) sc. Work to within 3(3,4) sc, ch 1, turn. Sl st across 4(4,4) sc, work to within 4(4,4) sc, ch 1, turn. Sl st across 4(4,4) sc, work to within 4(4,4) sc, ch 1, turn. Work 24(26,28) sc. End off.

Front

Work in same manner as back to armhole dec.

Shape Armhole and Neck: Sl st across 3(5,6) sc. Work 27(29,32) sc, ch 1, turn. Continue working rows of sc, dec'ing 1 sc at armhole edge every other row 4(5,6)x and 1 sc at neck edge every other row 12(13,14)x until armhole measures 7½ (8,8½) inches. 11(11,12) sc remain. End at armhole edge. Sl st across 3(4,4) sc. Work to neck edge, ch 1, turn. Work 4(4,4) sc. End off. Join yarn in next sc at base of V. Work in same manner as right side.

Join side seams and shoulders by overcasting.

Scenic vest color grid can be followed as is. But if you wish a stitch-by-stitch breakdown, follow the instructions under "Enlarging a Design" on page 30. Each square in the grids below represents 2½ inches.

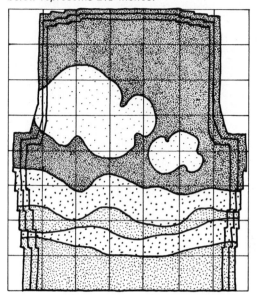

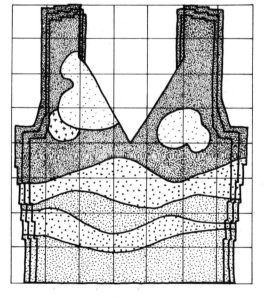

brown

green

blue

white

yellow

Armhole Trim: Attach yarn at underarm. Work 54(58,62) sc around armhole edge. Join with sl st, ch 1. Continue to work 1 sc in each sc, joining each rnd with a sl st and ch 1 until ½ inch has been worked.

Neck Trim: Attach yarn at shoulder seam. Work 31(33,35) sc along one side of neck edge and 31(33,35) sc along other half of neck edge. Work across back of neck. Join with a sl st and ch 1. Work 1 sc in each sc, dec'ing 1 st each side of center point every rnd for ¾ inch. End off.

Toast your toes in these cosy, fur-lined, after-ski slippers. Panel of leather on soles enables them to stand occasional outdoor wear. Design: Karen Cummings.

Toe Warmers

Fur-lined soles make these slipper socks cozy and warm. The slippers are worked in single crochet, from the top down. First you make a cylinder; then you work around the heel and across the top of the slipper to the toe.

Materials: Hand spun yarn, rug yarn weight: 1½ ounces *each* green, white, gold, purple
J aluminum crochet hook for sizes 5-6 and 7-8, K aluminum crochet hook for 9-10 (or hooks to give proper gauge)
Sheepskin for lining (piece large enough to cut 2 pieces 1 inch larger than soles)
Catalina leather (one square foot or piece large enough for 2 soles), available in leather supply stores
All-purpose contact rubber cement
Leather needle
Heavy-duty thread

Gauge: 3 stitches = 1 inch; 3 rows = 1 inch (for size 9-10, 5 stitches = 2 inches; 5 rows = 2 inches)

Main Stitch: Single crochet

Size: 5-6. Changes for 7-8, 9-10 in parentheses.

Starting at top, ch 30(30,31) for a length of approximately 12(12,12½) inches. Join with sl st to form circle. Continue sc around, following color chart and forming cylinder until piece measures 8(9,10) inches or desired height.

To Form Heel

Row 1: Join yarn to right side of last row at center front of boot, ch 2, sc in each st around (30 sc), ch 2, turn.

Row 2: Sc in each st across, ch 2, turn.

Row 3: Sc in 2nd st (dec made), sc across row, picking up last 2 sc tog (dec made, you now have 28 sc), ch 2, turn.

Row 4: Sc across. For size 5-6, end off and turn. (For sizes 7-8, 9-10, sc across a 5th row, end off, and turn.)

To Finish Heel, Instep and Toe

Row 1: On right side, join yarn where just ended off. Ch 2, sc in same sp, sc in each st around heel to corner, 2 sc in corner, sc across top of instep to corner [9(11,11) sc]. Join with sl st, ch 2.

Row 2: Continuing around in same direction on right side, sc in each st around heel to corner, ch 2. Working across top of instep, sc in end of last sc made and in each sc across row [13(15,15) sc across], ch 2, turn.

Working Toward Toe, Turning Each Row

Rows 3-6: Sc across row, ch 2, turn [13(15,15) sc].

Row 7: Sc across row, picking up last 2 sc tog [12(14,14) sc], ch 2, turn.

Row 8: Rep row 7 [11(13,13) sc].

Rows 9-10: Sc across row, ch 2, turn.

Row 11: Sc across row, picking up last 2 sc tog [10(12,12) sc].

Rows 12-13: Rep row 11 [8(10,10) sc]. For size 5-6, end off. For sizes 7-8, 9-10, rep row 11 (9 sc), end off.

To Finish: Sc around bottom edge. Using foot as pattern, cut catalina to size. Cut sheepskin 1 inch larger (all around) than catalina. With all-purpose contact rubber cement, glue skin side of sheepskin to wrong (rough) side of catalina. Shear furry side of sheepskin 1 inch around outer edge of catalina sole to prevent wrinkles when leather is sewn to tops. Using heavy-duty thread, sew slipper to sole.

Color Chart for Slippers

green	＋＋＋＋
white	▭▭▭▭
gold	✕✕✕✕
purple	●●●●

Necklace of Subdued Colors

This necklace of natural colors and soft, hand spun yarns is the perfect focal point for a dramatic evening dress or simple pants outfit. Any favorite found object — a shell, feathers, or bead — can serve as the centerpiece. Or you can substitute a small piece of driftwood for the bone bead we used.

For additional information on making tubes and medallions, see "Crocheting Geometric Shapes" (pages 32-33).

Materials: Leftover yarn scraps, or 1 ounce light brown sport weight wool yarn, hand spun if possible (color A); 1½ ounces dark brown sport weight yarn (color B); 1 ounce beige bulky weight yarn (color C)

G aluminum crochet hook (or hook to give proper gauge)

Gold-colored wire choker (available in craft and jewelry supply shops)

Brown heavy-duty thread or buttonhole twist

Yarn needle

Found object

Gauge: *Medallion:* 3 rounds = 1 inch; 3 stitches = 1 inch

Tubes: 4 rounds = 1 inch; 4 stitches = 1 inch

Size: Approximately 15 inches by 5 inches

Center of Necklace *(Medallion)*

With color C, ch 25, join with sl st to form ring.

Rnd 1: 25 sc.

Rnd 2: 1 sc in 1st sc, 2 sc in next sc, 1 sc in next sc, 2 sc in next sc. Work in this manner to end of rnd. Join with sl st. End off.

Rnd 3: With color A, ch 2, sk 1st st, sc in each st except where inc's are necessary to keep medallion flat. At these points (every 8 sts or so), work 2 sc in 1 st. At end of rnd, end off, leaving a long tail of yarn (about 1½ yards) to be used later.

Rnd 4: With color B, sc in each sc ¾ths of the way around medallion (approximately 35 sts). Then work 2 hdc, 2 dc, ch 2, 2 dc, 2 hdc, 8 sc, 2 hdc, 2 dc, ch 2, 2 hdc. Sl st to 1st color B sc. End off.

Top of Necklace *(Extension A)*

Count up 15 sts from last sl st, tie on color B, ch 13, turn.

Row 1: Sc in each ch, ch 2, turn.

Row 2: Sc in each sc, ch 2, turn.

Row 3: Sc in each sc. When you reach medallion, work one tr in sc next to where you joined yarn, then work 2 dc, 1 hdc, 2 sc.

Display a favorite shell *or bead in a dramatic necklace of warm colors. Design: Madge Copeland.*

Extension B

Ch 9, turn.

Row 1: 1 sc in each ch, ch 2, turn.

Row 2: 1 sc in each sc, ch 2, turn.

Row 3: 1 sc in each sc, attach to medallion with 1 sc, then work 2 sc, 1 hdc, 2 dc.

Extension C

Ch 13, turn.

Row 1: 1 sc in each ch, ch 2, turn.

Row 2: 1 sc in each sc to end of row. End off.

Tubes *(Long ones, make two)*

With color B, ch 9, join with sl st to form a ring. Sc in each st of ring, then continue to make a spiral tube by making 1 sc in each sc for 14 rnds (or until tube is 3½ inches long). End off, leaving about 8 inches of yarn to use to sew tube to medallion.

Short tube: Ch 9, join with sl st. Sc in each ch and around tube for 11 rnds (2½ inches long). End off, leaving an 8-inch tail of yarn.

To Join Tubes to Medallion: Thread needle with tail of yarn and sew each tube to medallion, with shorter tube in middle.

Tassels *(Make three):* Cut a few 12-inch strands of each color of yarn. Tie at top with heavy-duty thread. Thread a tassel into middle of each tube and sew invisibly near where tube joins medallion. Trim ends of tassels.

Centerpiece: With heavy-duty thread and yarn needle, attach found object to center of medallion. Thread wire choker through ends of rows of extensions.

Packable Purses of Jute

Jute in a variety of colors was our choice of materials for these two purses, but heavy natural yarn or synthetic rug yarn would also work well.

Since the weight of jute varies considerably, you may have trouble getting exactly the same gauge prescribed in the instructions. If this is the case, plan on a slightly larger or smaller purse.

Carryall Purse

Materials: 10 ounces of 3-ply jute or macramé twine: 7 ounces color A (natural); 1 ounce *each* color B (aqua), color C (rust), color D (brown)
K aluminum crochet hook (or hook to give proper gauge)
Gauge: 2 stitches = 1 inch; 3 rows = 1 inch
Main Stitch: Single crochet

With color A, ch 26.
Row 1: Sc in 2nd ch from hook and in each ch to end (25 sc), ch 1, turn.
Rows 2-35: Sc in 1st sc and in each sc across row, ch 1, turn.
Row 36: Sc in 1st sc and in each sc across row.
Row 37: Join color B in last st, ch 1, sc in each sc across row, ch 1, turn.
Row 38: Rep row 36.
Row 39: With color A, rep row 37.
Row 40: Rep row 36.
Row 41: With color C, rep row 37.
Row 42: With color A, rep row 37.
Row 43: Rep row 35.
Row 44: Rep row 36.
Row 45: With color D, rep row 37.
Rows 46-49: Rep row 35.
Row 50: With color A, rep row 37.
Row 51: Rep row 36.
Row 52: With color C, rep row 37.
Row 53: Rep row 36.
Row 54: With color A, rep row 37.
Row 55: Rep row 36. Piece should measure approximately 11½ inches by 22 inches.

To Finish: Fold piece in two width wise with right side out. Hold piece with fold at bottom (fold is right side seam). Join color A at upper right corner and, working across side to corner, sc evenly through both thicknesses, forming a seam (25 sc). Work 3 sc in corner sp. Continue in same manner across bottom edge (27 sc), ch 1, turn. Sc back across previous row, ch 4, turn. Working again along bottom, sk 2 sts, sl st into next st, * ch 4, sk 2 sts, sl st in next st, rep from * 7x (9 lps), turn. Sl st to middle of last lp, ** ch 4, sl st into sp of next lp, rep from ** across (8 lps). End off.

To Finish Top Edge: Join color A at corner, sc evenly around top edge, join with sl st. End off.

To Make Strap: Ch 65 (or desired length), turn, sc in 2nd ch and in each ch across row to end, ch 1, turn. * sc in 1st sc and in each sc across row, ch 1, turn. Rep from * across (or to desired width). Sew straps evenly to corners of purse.

Flap Top Purse

Materials: Macramé twine: 131 yards natural (color A), 30 yards purple (color B), 13 yards aqua (color C)
K aluminum crochet hook (or hook to give proper gauge)
¾-inch ceramic bead
Gauge: 3 stitches = 1 inch; 2 rows = 1½ inches
Main Stitch: Half double crochet

To Shape Body of Purse
With color A, ch 47.
Row 1: Hdc in 3rd ch from hook, hdc in each ch until last st, 5 hdc in last st to turn and continue hdc around, picking up other side of each ch. End off.
Row 2: In top of last st, join color B, ch 2. Hdc in between each st across row until 1st sp of 5 hdc group, 2 hdc in each of next 4 sps, continue hdc in between each st to end of row. End off.
Row 3: Join color A to top of last st, ch 2, hdc in each sp across until 1st 2 hdc sp. 2 hdc in that sp, * hdc in next sp, 2 hdc in next sp, rep from * 2x; hdc in each sp to end, ch 2, turn.
Row 4: Hdc in each sp across until 1st 2 hdc sp, 2 hdc in that sp, * hdc in next 2 sps, 2 hdc in next sp, rep from * 2x; hdc in each sp to end of row. End off.
Row 5: Join color C to top of last st, ch 2, hdc in each sp across until 1st 2 hdc sp. 2 hdc in that sp, * hdc in next 3 sps, 2 hdc in next sp, rep from * 2x; hdc in each sp to end of row. End off.
Row 6: Join color A in top of last st, ch 2, hdc in each sp across row until 1st 2 hdc sp. 2 hdc in that sp, * hdc in next 4 sps, 2 hdc in next sp, rep from * 2x; hdc in each sp to end of row, ch 2, turn.
Row 7: Hdc in each sp to 1st 2 hdc sp, 2 hdc in that sp, * hdc in next 5 sps, 2 hdc in next sp, rep from * 2x, hdc in each remaining sp to end, ch 2, turn.
Before making row 8, make latch hole by counting 3 sps from 2nd 2 hdc sp in previous row. Join color B, ch 10, join with sl st to next sp (lp should be centered on flap), ch 2, sk sp, sl st in next sp, turn, 11 hdc into lp made by ch 10, attached with sl st to

Flap Top Purse
Ceramic bead *makes clever latch for tricolor flap top purse. Bag is crocheted in two pieces — one piece forms the front, back, and flap of the purse; the other serves as a combination strap and side panel. Design: Karen Cummings.*

flap in 2nd sp from where color B was originally joined. End off.

Row 8: Hdc in each sp to 1st 2 hdc sp, 2 hdc in that sp, hdc in next 6 sps, 2 hdc in next sp. To work around latch hole, * in next sp (where color B attached), yo, draw lp through sp, keep on hook. Working on latch, rep from * 2x, yo, draw through 7 lps on hook (corner made). Work around latch, making 2 hdc in each sp 8x. At corner ** in next sp, yo, draw lp through sp, keep on hook, rep from ** 2x. Yo, draw through 7 lps of hook, 2 hdc in next sp, hdc in next 6 sps, 2 hdc in next sp (should be on top of 2 hdc sp of previous row); hdc in each sp to end of row. End off.

To Make Strap: With color A, ch 82.

Row 1: 2 hdc in 3rd ch from hook, hdc in each st until last st, 5 hdc in last st to turn and continue hdc around, picking up other side of each ch. In last st, work 2 more hdc, join with sl st. End off.

Row 2: Join color B and work as in row 1, making hdc in each sp along sides and at each end and 2 hdc in each of the four 2 hdc sps of previous row. Join with sl st. End off.

Row 3: Join color A, work as on rows 1 and 2 along sides. At each end, work as follows: in 1st 2 hdc sps, make 2 hdc, * hdc in next sp, 2 hdc in next sp, rep from * 2x. Join with sl st. End off.

To Finish: Set strap in evenly, using sl st to seam. For latch, attach ceramic bead to body with color A.

Carryall Purse
Striped and sturdy *tote bag made of jute is super simple to crochet. Design: Karen Cummings.*

Waist Accents

(Color photo on facing page)

Belts no longer just hold up your pants. Now they are decorative accents — a kind of "jewelry" for your waist. These can be made to fit anyone, any size, from Junior in his jeans to Grandma in her girdle.

Leather and Linen Belt

Materials: Strip of leather (any width; length should be waist or hip measurement plus 5 inches or more for overlap and 2 inches fold back for buckle)
About 36 yards of 3-ply linen (sold on a tube) or fine macramé twine
Purchased buckle and rivets
Leather punch
O steel crochet hook (or hook to give proper gauge)
Gauge: 1 sc, 1 ch = ½ inch; 1 row = ½ inch
Main Stitch: Single crochet

With scissors, slightly round flap end of leather. Mark belt ¼ inch in from edge at ½-inch intervals along entire length on both edges. Using leather punch, punch holes large enough to allow O hook to penetrate easily.

Join linen or twine to top edge of leather at buckle end. Work along edge making * 1 sc through each hole, ch 1, rep from * across to last hole at rounded end; in last hole make 3 sc, ch 1. Working along opposite edge, make 3 sc in 1st hole, ch 1, ** 1 sc through hole, ch 1, rep from ** across to buckle end, ch 1, turn. Sc in each sc of previous row, placing 2 sc in 2nd sc of group of 3 sc at corners.

To Finish: Insert belt through buckle, fold back leather 1 to 2 inches. Use post or rivet to secure flap, and, with needle and thread, slip stitch flap to belt. Punch hole in appropriate place for buckle.

Leather Lacing Belt

Materials: Leather lace ⅛ inch wide. (Approximately 25 yards of ⅛-inch lace will make a belt 2 inches wide and 28 to 30 inches long.)
Purchased buckle
H aluminum crochet hook (or hook to give proper gauge)
Main Stitch: Double crochet
Gauge: 3 stitches = 1 inch; 1 row = 1 inch

Ch 3.
Row 1: 2 dc in 1st ch, ch 3, turn.
Row 2: 2 dc in next 2 sts (5 sts), ch 3, turn.
Row 3: Dc in *back* lp of each st (see page 72) across

one row and in *front* lp of each st across the next row. Continue to alternate back and front, ending each row with ch 3, turn.

To Finish: When belt is almost the desired length, stretch it by pulling on it. Because of the tension, belt may stretch or give with wear, so allow for this when working to finished length. When you have the desired length, add buckle to belt with slip stitch or wrap leather around buckle and then through a stitch all the way across. Weave in ends.

Knobby Woolen Belt

Made in an unconventional manner, this belt begins with a core (the chain) and you work out from there. Succeeding rows are done around this core — that is, you work down the top length of the belt, around one end, down the other length (the bottom of the belt), and around the other end, making a rectangle.

Materials: One 4-ounce skein of wool knitting worsted in *each* color: color A, pink; color B, gold; color C, rose; color D, blue; color E, red
H aluminum crochet hook (or hook to give proper gauge)
Two ⅝-inch buttons or bells
Gauge: 4 sc stitches = 1 inch
Main Stitch: Single crochet
Size: 4½ inches wide; adjustable length

Measure around hips. With color A, make a ch that is 4 or 5 inches shorter than hip measurement (we made a ch of 100 sts for a belt 30 inches long).
Row 1: Sc in 2nd ch from hook and in each ch across, 2 sc in last ch, ch 1, turn. Sc in each ch across, picking up other side of each ch, 2 sc in last ch.
Row 2: With color B, * work one popcorn stitch (see page 75 for popcorn stitch), 1 sc, rep from * across 1st row. 2 sc in corner, turn and rep pat (1 popcorn st, 1 sc) across bottom of row to other corner. Work 2 sc in corner.
Row 3: Sc all the way around row 2, inc'ing two sts at both corners. Finish off with a sl st.
Row 4: With color C, sc all the way around row 3, inc'ing 2 sts at each corner. Finish off with a sl st.
Row 5: Work * 1 sc, 1 dc, ch 1, sk 1 st, rep from * all the way around, working a ch 3 in each corner. End row with a sl st.
Rows 6-7: With color D, rep pat from * on row 5 across length of last row. At end of row, tie off color D (do not go across end of belt). Attach color D to one end of the color C row. Rep row 5 from * across length of belt. Tie off color D at end of row (do not go across other end).
Row 8: With color E, sc along length of belt, 2 sc in corner, sc across end of belt, 2 sc in corner, sc in each st along bottom of belt, 2 sc in corner, 4 sc, ch 2 (this makes a buttonhole), sk 2 sts, 6 sc, ch 2 (2nd buttonhole), sk 2 sts, 4 sc, join with sl st. Sew on buttons or bells to match up with buttonholes.

Belts *for the entire family are pictured above. Designs: Leather and linen belt, Karen Cummings; knobby woolen belt, Pamela Hinchcliffe; leather lacing belt, Tina Kauffman. Instructions on facing page.*

Bike-riding businessman *will appreciate a casual tweedy tie made of single crochet with a slip stitch border. Use the tweed yarn indicated or substitute two contrasting strands of thin yarn. Design: Lynne Morrall.*

Necktie, Irish Style

Begin this Irish tweed tie by starting at the point at the bottom front of tie. You form a triangle and then decrease to the width of the band around the neck. You then continue to decrease until you reach the point at the other end.

Materials: Approximately 180 yards of single-ply light weight Irish Donegal tweed, 3-ply cotton, or other yarn of similar weight and texture
H aluminum crochet hook (or hook to give proper gauge)
Gauge: 8 stitches and 8 rows = 2 inches
Main Stitch: Single crochet
Finished Length: 56 inches

Ch 2.
Row 1: Insert hook into 1st ch, work 1 sc. Ch 1, turn. (Ch 1, turn at the end of each row.)
Row 2: 3 sc in the 1 sc.
Row 3: 2 sc in 1st sc of row 2, 1 sc in 2nd st, 2 sc in 3rd st.
Rows 4-10: Work as in rows 1-3, inc'ing at the ends of each row by putting two sts in the 1st and last st.
Rows 11-13: Sc in each sc (19 sts).

Row 14: (Begin dec) sc in each sc, dec'ing in 1st and last st (17 sts).
Rows 15-17: Sc in each sc (17 sts).
Row 18: Rep row 14 (15 sts).
Rows 19-48: Sc in each sc (15 sts).
Row 49: Rep row 14 (13 sts).
Rows 50-68: Sc in each sc (13 sts).
Row 69: Rep row 14 (11 sts).
Rows 70-89: Sc in each sc (11 sts).
Row 90: Rep row 14 (9 sts).
Rows 91-100: Sc in each sc (9 sts).
Row 101: Rep row 14 (7 sts).
Rows 102-113: Sc in each sc (7 sts).
Row 114: Rep row 14 (5 sts).
Rows 115-209: Sc in each sc (5 sts).
Row 210: Sc in each sc, inc'ing 1 st in 1st st and in last st (7 sts).
Rows 211-225: Sc in each sc (7 sts).
Rows 226-228: Rep row 14 (1 st).
Row 229: Sc in last sc.

To Finish: Sc all around outside of tie, ch 1 at corners and at points to keep tie from puckering. Then sl st around tie in each sc and each ch. Block tie.

A Covey of Caps

Hats for many occasions — riding, driving, skiing, or simply "showing off" — are featured here. Since all the hats are quite stretchy and flexible, one size fits everybody.

All the hats are made from the crown down to the brim, and all begin with a ring. After slip stitching the chain together to form a ring, you crochet into the ring to form a circle which will "grow" to become the crown of the hat.

Peruvian-style Hat

You begin at the crown of the hat and make a spiral (rather than individual rounds) of single crochet. After changing to the third color, you work in rounds of single and double crochet. The contrasting edging is a long, single-crochet tube, slip stitched to the hat.

Materials: 1 ounce lavender bulky weight hand spun wool (color A), 1 ounce purple fine weight hand spun wool (color B), 2 ounces pink bulky weight hand spun wool (color C)
I and F aluminum crochet hooks (or hooks to give proper gauge)
Heavy-duty thread
Yarn needle
Gauge: 3 sc stitches = 1 inch, 2 sc rows = 1 inch; 5 dc stitches = 2 inches, 5 dc rows = 4 inches
Main Stitch: Double crochet

Step 1: With color A and with I hook, ch 4, join with sl st to form ring.
Step 2: 5 sc in ring.
Step 3: (2 sc in next st, 3 sc)5x.
Step 4: 20 sc. Change to color B on last yo of last sc.
Step 5: (3 sc, 2 sc in next sc)6x.
Step 6: 20 sc. Change to color C on last yo of last sc.
Rnd 1: (3 sc, 2 sc in next st)7x.
Rnd 2: 25 dc.
Rnd 3: (4 dc, 2 dc in next dc)5x.
Rnd 4: 30 dc.
Rnd 5: (5 dc, 2 dc in next dc)4x.
Rnd 6: (5 dc, 2 dc in next dc)5x, 5 dc.
Rnd 7: 41 dc. Change to color A on last yo of last dc.
Rnd 8: (5 dc, 2 dc in next dc)6x, 5 dc.
Rnd 9: (5 dc, 2 dc in next dc)7x, 5 dc.
Rnd 10: 54 sc, ch 1, turn.
Rnd 11: 28 sc. Add color C on last yo of last sc, ch 1, turn. (You are now working with 2 strands of yarn.)
Rnd 12: 28 sc, ch 1, turn.
Rnd 13: 28 sc. End off.

Edging

Step 1: With color B and with F hook, ch 4, join with sl st to form ring.
Step 2: Form a single crochet spiral tube the length of the perimeter of the bottom edge of the hat by crocheting around the ring without inc'ing or dec'ing to the desired length.
Step 3: Make 2 more spiral tubes, each 10 inches long. Sew these to the ear flaps with heavy-duty sewing thread.
Step 4: Pin long edging tube to bottom of hat, sl st to hat with matching yarn (color B) and F hook. End off.

Green Tyrolian Hat

Wouldn't this Tyrolian-style hat make a perfect Father's Day or Christmas gift for Dad or Grandad?

Crochet as tightly as possible and the texture of the hat will be like a sturdy, tightly woven fabric that can be shaped and molded to reflect its fashionable wearer's personality.

Materials: Two 4-ounce skeins green 4-ply orlon (or substitute 3 strands of 3-ply yarn. For a tweed effect, use 3 different 3-ply yarns)
J and H aluminum crochet hooks (or hooks to give proper gauge)
Yarn needle
Gauge: 4 stitches = 1 inch; 3 rounds = 1 inch
Main Stitch: Single crochet

With J hook and 2 strands of 4-ply (or 3 strands of 3-ply) yarn held together, ch 4. Join with sl st to form ring.
Rnd 1: 6 sc in ring. Place a marker in last sc (scrap of yarn may be tied to sc for a marker) to indicate where new rnd begins.
Rnd 2: 2 sc in each sc in rnd 1 (inc made in every st). (12 sts in rnd 2).
Rnd 3: * 1 sc in next sc, 2 sc in next sc (inc made). Rep from * all around.
Rnd 4: * 1 sc in next 2 sc, 2 sc in next sc (inc made). Rep from * all around.
Rnd 5: Sc all around, inc'ing every 4th sc.
Rnds 6-11: Sc all around, inc'ing in every inc of previous rnd (6 sts inc'd in each rnd). At end of rnd 11, 66 sc in rnd.
Rnds 12-26: Sc in each sc. (If you want a higher crown, add more rnds of sc at this point.)

Shape Brim (Made in rows of dc)

Rnd 1: Ch 3 (for 1st dc), 2 dc in both lps of next sc (inc made); dc all around, inc'ing 1 dc in every other sc. To end this and all rnds of brim, sl st in top of 3rd ch.
Rnd 2: Ch 3 (for 1st dc), dc in each dc to end of rnd.

Like birds of a feather, hat lovers flock together. Instructions for all five caps are on pages 50-53. Designs: Peruvian-style hat (far left), Nancy Copeland; green Tyrolian hat, H. Louyse Younger; yellow cloche hat, Nancy Lipe; cowboy hat, Lynne Streeter; reversible ski hat, Tina Kauffman.

Rnds 3-4: Rep rnd 2 of brim. (If you want a larger brim, dc more rnds. However, you'll have to inc more dc to keep the work flat.) End brim with sl st in top of 3rd ch.

Cut yarn, leaving ends long enough to thread through needle. Neatly weave ends into work.

Band

With H hook and 2 strands of yarn, ch 5, turn.

Row 1: Sc in 2nd ch from hook and in each ch to end, ch 1, turn.

Row 2 and all other rows: Sc in 2nd sc and in each sc to end of row, ch 1, turn. Continue to work rows of sc until band is 24 inches long (or desired length). Cut yarn, leaving ends long enough to use for sewing the band together. Slip band over crown. Tack down if you wish.

Yellow Cloche Cap

To create the unusual pattern stitch, you use a double strand of yarn and put succeeding rows of double crochet in the chain-1 space or between the two double crochets of the previous row of stitches.

Materials: 3 ounces yellow mohair or mohair/acrylic yarn

J and I aluminum crochet hooks (or hooks to give proper gauge)

Yarn needle

Gauge: 5 dc = 2 inches; 3 rows = 2 inches

Main Stitch: Double crochet

(Continued on next page)

PROJECTS  51

With double strand of yarn and J hook, ch 4, sl st to form a ring.

Rnd 1: (Ch 1, dc into ring)12x. Mark end of row with colored thread.

Rnd 2: 2 dc into 1st sp, ch 1, 2 dc into 2nd sp, ch 1, 2 dc into 3rd sp. Continue around to end of rnd.

Rnd 3: 2 dc into 1st sp, 2 dc into 2nd sp, 2 dc into 3rd sp. Continue around to end of rnd. (This rnd is identical to rnd 2, except no chs are made.)

Rnds 4-9: 2 dc in between the dc of the previous rnd, sk the hole, 2 dc into the 2nd dc, sk the next hole, continue to work in this manner to end of rnd 9.

To Finish: Work one rnd of loose sc. Close rnd with a sl st.

Flower (Made in three pieces)

Flower A: With single strand of yarn and I hook, ch 6, join with sl st to form ring.

Rnd 1: Ch 5 (dc in ring, ch 2)5x to create 6 sps. Sl st in 3rd ch of the ch-5.

Rnd 2: (Ch 7, 1 sc in 2nd ch between dc's)6x to create 6 sps.

Rnd 3: Over each lp, work 1 sc, 1 hdc, 2 dc, 4 tr, 5 dbl tr, 4 tr, 2 dc, 1 hdc, 1 sc. Sl st and end off.

Flower B: Ch 6, join with sl st to form a ring.

Rnd 1: Ch 5 (dc in ring, ch 2)5x to create 6 sps, sl st in 3rd ch of the ch-5.

Rnd 2: (Ch 7, sc in 2nd ch between dc's)6x to create 6 sps.

Rnd 3: Over each lp work 1 sc, 1 hdc, 2 dc, 9 tr, 2 dc, 1 hdc, 1 sc. Sl st and end off.

Flower C: Ch 6, join with sl st to form ring.

Rnd 1: Ch 5 (dc in ring, ch 2)5x to create 6 sps. Sl st in 3rd ch of the ch-5.

Rnd 2: In each sp work 1 sc, 1 hdc, 4 dc, 1 hdc, 1 sc until 6 petals are made. Join with sl st.

Rnd 3: (Ch 7, 1 sc in between petals)6x. Sl st to 1st ch-7.

Rnd 4: Over the 1st 3 ch-7s, work 1 sc, 1 hdc, 8 dc, 1 hdc, 1 sc. Over the next 3 ch-7s, work 1 sc, 1 hdc, 8 dc, 1 hdc, 1 sc. Over the next 3 ch-7s, work 1 sc, 1 hdc, 2 dc, 4 tr, 5 dbl tr, 4 tr, 2 dc, 1 hdc, 1 sc. Sl st, end off.

To join flowers: Place flower A right side up. Place the center of flower B (right side up) on top of and centered over flower A.

Place flower C (right side up) on flat surface. Fold flower C in half with the 3 *small* outside petals over the 3 *large* outside petals. Pull the center petals together and tie together with yarn along center fold.

Place the folded flower C on top of and centered over flower B.

Sew the 3 flowers together. Then place the 3 flowers on the hat and sew to the hat, using a yarn needle and the same yarn.

Cowboy Hat

The unique cowboy shape is achieved by crocheting extremely tight and even stitches. You work the hat in three parts: crown, band, and brim. Since the size of the band is flexible, decrease as necessary for a good fit. Be sure to stagger the places where you begin each yarn (to prevent a seam from showing) and slip stitch at the end of each round to keep the rounds the same height.

Materials: Bulky hand spun yarns: 4 ounces gray alpaca and wool (color A), 4 ounces gray wool (color B), 1 ounce cream wool (color C), 1 ounce dark brown wool with either angora or mohair (either 2 yarns held together or one yarn spun of the 2 fibers) (color D), 1 ounce dark brown wool (color E), 1 ounce charcoal gray wool with either angora or mohair (either 2 yarns held together or one yarn spun of the 2 fibers) (color F)
F aluminum crochet hook (or hook to give proper gauge)
Yarn needle

Gauge: 6 stitches = 2 inches, 5 rows = 2 inches (crown and brim); 8 rows = 2 inches (band)

Main Stitch: Crown: half double crochet; band and brim: single crochet

Crown

Rnd 1: With color A, ch 4, sl st to form ring, ch 2. (Be sure to sl st at end of *each* rnd.)

Rnd 2: 10 hdc in ring, ch 2.

Rnd 3: 2 hdc in each st, ch 2.

Placement of flowers for cloche hat

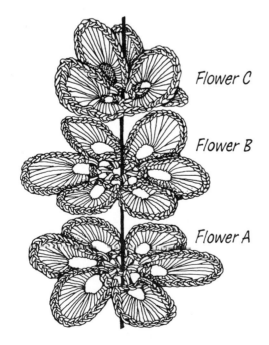

Flower C

Flower B

Flower A

Rnd 4: Hdc in each st, inc'ing in every other st, ch 2.

Rnd 5: Hdc in each st, inc'ing in every 3rd st; ch 2.

Rnd 6: Hdc in each st, inc'ing in every 4th st; ch 2.

Rnd 7: Hdc in each st, inc'ing in every 5th st; ch 2.

Rnd 8: Hdc in each st, inc'ing twice (evenly spaced); ch 2.

Rnds 9-12: Hdc in each st; ch 2.

Rnd 13: Hdc in each st, inc'ing twice (evenly spaced); ch 2.

Rnd 14: Hdc in each st. End off.

Rnd 15: Tie on color B, ch 2, hdc in each st, ch 2.

Rnds 16-17: Hdc in each st, ch 2.

Rnd 18: Hdc in each st. End off.

Band

Rnd 1: Tie on color C, 1 sc in each st. (Be sure to sl st at end of *each* rnd.) End off.

Rnd 2: Tie on color D, ch 1, 1 sc in each st, dec'ing 2 sts (evenly spaced) if needed for a good fit. End off.

Rnd 3: Tie on color E, ch 1, 1 sc in each st, ch 1.

Rnd 4: 1 sc in each st, dec'ing 1 or 2 sts (evenly spaced) if needed for a good fit. End off.

Rnd 5: Tie on color F, ch 1, 1 sc in each st. End off.

Rnd 6: Tie on color E, ch 1, 1 sc in each st, ch 1.

Rnd 7: 1 sc in each st. End off.

Rnd 8: Tie on color D, ch 1, 1 sc in each st. End off.

Brim

Rnd 1: Tie on color C, ch 1, 2 sc in each st. (Be sure to sl st at end of *each* rnd.) End off.

Rnd 2: Tie on color A, ch 1, 1 sc in each st.

Rnds 3-7: Ch 1, 1 sc in each st.

Rnd 8: Ch 1, 1 sc in each st, inc'ing 2 sts (evenly spaced). End off.

Rnd 9: Tie on color B, ch 1, 1 sc in each st.

Rnd 10: Ch 1, 1 sc in each st. End off. Block brim if necessary to even the shaping.

Reversible Ski Hat

Skiers and other cold-weather sportsmen will keep their ears warm in this double layer hat. The pompon goes through to the inside, adding a finishing touch to both sides of the reversible cap.

Materials: Acrylic knitting worsted, one 4-ounce skein of *each* color: blue, green, red
E aluminum crochet hook (or hook to give proper gauge)
Yarn needle

Gauge: 4 stitches = 1 inch; 2 rows = 1 inch

Main Stitch: Double crochet

Note: Follow the color chart at right for the necessary color changes.

Ch 28. Join with sl st to form a ring.

Rnd 1: Dc in each st around (28 sts). Join with sl st, ch 3.

Rnd 2: Begin inc. Each rnd will be inc'd by 4 sts, worked evenly around (avoid placing inc's directly on top of each other). * Dc in each of next 6 sts, 2 dc in 7th st, rep from * around. Join with sl st to 1st st to form rnd (32 sts).

Rnd 3: Ch 3, * dc in each of next 7 sts, 2 dc in 8th st, rep from * around. Join with sl st to first st (36 sts).

Rnd 4: Ch 3. Rep rnd 3, inc'ing every 9th st (40 sts).

Rnds 5-14: Continue to inc 4 sts evenly around each rnd until you have 80 sts.

Rnds 15-26: Dc in each st around.

Rnds 27-40: Dec each rnd by 4 sts in the same manner as inc'ing. End off.

Pompon: Wrap yarn around a 4-inch piece of cardboard 150 times. Slip yarn off cardboard and tie a piece of yarn tightly around center. Snip loops at both ends.

To Finish: Fold hat in half at center line (see color chart). Sew together along side seam, using a yarn needle and overcast stitch. Fold hat in half crosswise by stuffing one side into the other. Stitch ends of hat together at top, leaving an opening in the center for the pompon. Gather pompon into two equal sections and push into hole until it's halfway through. Fold cuff back.

Ski hat color chart

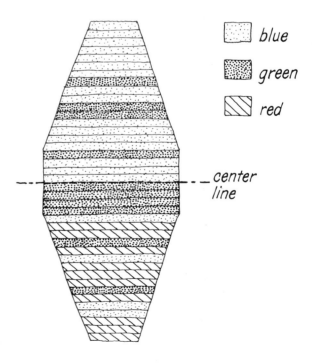

blue

green

red

center line

Turtleneck Chic

The outdoorsman in your life will enjoy wearing this warm, acrylic turtleneck made by a simple combination of one single crochet and one chain stitch.

Materials: 5(6,6,7) 4-ounce skeins of burnt orange 4-ply acrylic knitting worsted
F and I aluminum crochet hooks (or hooks to give proper gauge)
Yarn needle
Gauge: Single crochet: 3½ stitches = 1 inch, 4 rows = 1 inch; Pattern stitch: 11 stitches = 3 inches, 3½ rows = 1 inch
Main Stitch: Single crochet
Size: Small (36), Medium (38), Large (40-42), Extra Large (44)

Back

With F hook, ch 62(66,74,76) loosely to measure 17(18,20,21) inches.

Ribbing

Row 1: Sc in 2nd ch from hook and in each ch across, ch 1, turn. You will have 61(65,73,75) sc.

Row 2: Sc in 1st sc and in each sc across, ch 1, turn. Rep this row until you have 3 inches for ribbing.

Pattern Stitch

Row 1: With I hook, sc in 1st sc, * ch 1, sk 1 sc, sc in next sc, rep from * across. Ch 1, turn.

Row 2: Sc in 1st sc, * ch 1, sc in next sc, rep from * across, ch 1, turn. Rep this row for 4(2,3,3) inches.

Begin Increasing: Work inc's every 4(2,3,3) inches 2(4,4,4)x. (Work inc's as follows: First inc: 2 sc in 1st and last sc of row; second inc: 1 sc, ch 1, 1 sc in 1st and last sc of row; third inc: same as 1st inc; fourth inc: same as 2nd inc.) Continue in pat st until piece measures 15(15,16,16) inches from bottom of ribbing or to desired length to underarm.

Underarm Decrease: Sl st across 4(4,6,6) sts. (Sl st across 1st sc, 1st ch, 2nd sc, 2nd ch for small and medium sizes. Sl across 1st sc and 1st ch, 2nd sc, 2nd ch, 3rd sc, 3rd ch for large and extra large sizes.) Ch 1, sc in next sc. Work in pat across row, stopping short of 2 sc and 2 ch for small and medium sizes and 3 sc and 3 ch for large and extra large sizes.

Raglan Decreases: 1st dec: Work sc in 1st sc, sc in 2nd sc. Work in pat to 2nd sc from end. Sc in 2nd sc from end, sc in last sc. You have omitted one ch between 1st two sc and last two sc (dec of 2 sts).
2nd dec: Insert hook into 1st sc, yo, pull through, insert hook into 2nd sc, yo, draw through 3 lps on hook. Work in pat st across row to last 2 sc, draw up a lp in next sc, draw up a lp in last sc, yo, draw through 3 lps on hook.

Continue in pat and work dec's every other row 10(9,8,9)x. Then work dec's every row 8(13,16,15)x. End off; 19(21,21,23) sts remain for neck.

Front

Work same as for back to underarm dec. Work underarm dec same as for back for 18(20,22,22) rows above beginning of underarm dec. Continue to dec at arm edge and work across 16(18,17,19) sts, sk 7 sts (for neck), work in pat across row.

Neck dec: Continue to dec at armhole as in raglan dec's and, at the same time, dec one st at neck edge every row 6(7,7,8)x. End off.

Sleeves (Make 2)

With F hook, ch 30(32,32,34) to measure 8(8½,8½,9) inches.

Row 1: Sc in 2nd ch from hook and in each ch across, ch 1, turn. You have 29(31,31,33) sc. Rep for 3 inches. With I hook, work in pat, inc'ing evenly across row to 39(39,39,43) sts (remember the ch 1 counts as a st). Working in pat st, inc as above 1 st each end every 6(5,6,6) rows 2(11,1,3)x; then every 5(0,5,5) rows 8(0,10,8)x. Continue until desired length of underarm.

Sl st across 4(4,6,6) sts. Work in pat, dec'ing (raglan dec's) each end every other row 6(8,11,10)x, then every row 16(15,10,13)x. End off. 7 sts remain.

To Finish: Join front and back and sleeves by overcasting. Begin at center back and work 1 row sc around neck edge. Ch 1, turn. Work in pat st around neck, ch 1, turn at end of each rnd. Work 5 inches (or more) of pat st for turtleneck. Sew neck seam.

Sailors, skiers, and scavengers *could warm up to this turtleneck nicely. Design: Katherine Dauth.*

Rug & Pillow

(Color photo on page 56)

Native American Indian designs inspired the creator of this 3½ by 5-foot throw rug and matching pillow. We used Mexican wool yarn, but any yarn of similar weight (such as rug yarn) could be substituted. Natural, earthy colors seem best suited for this traditional design.

Throw Rug

Materials: *Rug:* Heavy weight Mexican hand spun yarn or rug yarn: 1¾ pounds color A (brown), 6 ounces *each* color B (orange), color C (green), color D (yellow). *Pillow:* 4 ounces of each of the rug colors
Stuffing material for pillow: purchased pillow form, or dacron or cotton batting, or shredded foam and lining material (½ yard of 36-inch or 45-inch fabric)
J aluminum crochet hook (or hook to give proper gauge)
Gauge: 5 stitches = 2 inches; 3 rows = 2 inches
Size: *Rug:* Approximately 40 by 60 inches (without fringe); *Pillow:* 14 inches square
Main Stitch: Double crochet

With color A, ch 82
Row 1: Dc in 2nd ch, dc in next 80 sts, ch 3, turn.

Row 2: Sk 1 st, dc in next 79 sts, ch 3, turn.

Row 3: Rep row 2.

Row 4: Sk 1 st, dc in next 4 sts; * with color B, dc in next 10 sts; with color A, dc in next 5 sts, rep from * 4x, ch 3, turn.

Row 5: Rep row 4.

Row 6: Sk 1 st, dc in next 4 sts; * with color B, dc in next 6 sts; with color A, dc in next 9 sts; rep from * 4x, ch 3, turn.

Row 7: Sk 1 st, dc in next 8 sts; * with color B, dc in next 6 sts; with color A, dc in next 9 sts; rep from * 3x; with color B, dc in next 6 sts; with color A, dc in next 5 sts; (carry A along through whole rug rather than tying it off), ch 3, turn.

Row 8: With color B, sk 1 st, dc in next 79 sts, ch 3, turn.

Row 9: Sk 1 st, dc in next 79 sts; ch 3, turn, tie off color B.

Rows 10-11: With color A, sk 1 st, dc in next 79 sts, ch 3, turn.

Rows 12-19: Rep rows 4-11, using color C instead of color B. (Tie off color C at end of row 17.)

Rows 20-27: Rep rows 4-11, using color D instead of color B. At end of row 27, tie on color B, ch 3, turn. (At end of row 25, tie off color D.)

Row 28: Sk 1 st, dc in next 79 sts, ch 3, turn.

Row 29: Sk 1 st, dc in next 79 sts, tie off color B and tie on color C, ch 3, turn.

Row 30: Sk 1 st, dc in next 79 sts, ch 3, turn.

Row 31: Sk 1 st, dc in next 79 sts, tie off color C and tie on color D, ch 3, turn.

Row 32: Sk 1 st, dc in next 79 sts, ch 3, turn.

Row 33: Sk 1 st, dc in next 79 sts, with color A, ch 3, turn.

Row 34: Sk 1 st, dc in next 79 sts, ch 3, turn.

Row 35: Sk 1 st, dc in next 79 sts; with color D, ch 3, turn.

Row 36: Sk 1 st, dc in next 79 sts, ch 3, turn.

Row 37: Sk 1 st, dc in next 79 sts; tie off color D, tie on color C, ch 3, turn.

Row 38: Sk 1 st, dc in next 79 sts, ch 3, turn.

Row 39: Sk 1 st, dc in next 79 sts; tie off color C and tie on color B, ch 3, turn.

Row 40: Sk 1 st, dc in next 79 sts, ch 3, turn.

Row 41: Sk 1 st, dc in next 79 sts; tie off color B; with color A, ch 3, turn.

Row 42: Sk 1 st, dc in next 79 sts, ch 3, turn.

Row 43: Sk 1 st, dc in next 79 sts; tie on color D, ch 3, turn.

Row 44: Sk 1st, dc in next 79 sts, ch 3, turn.

Row 45: Sk 1 st, dc in next 79 sts; with color A, ch 3, turn.

Row 46: Sk 1 st, dc in next 8 sts; * with color D, dc in next 6 sts; with color A, dc in next 9 sts; rep from * 3x; with color D, dc in next 6 sts; with color A, dc in next 5 sts, ch 3, turn.

Row 47: Sk 1 st, dc in next 4 sts; * with color D, dc in next 6 sts; with color A, dc in next 9 sts; rep from * 4x, ch 3, turn.

Row 48: Sk 1 st, dc in next 4 sts; * with color D, dc in next 10 sts; with color A, dc in next 5 sts; rep from * 4x; ch 3, turn.

Row 49: Rep row 48. Tie off color D.

Rows 50-57: Rep rows 42-49, using color C instead of color D. Tie off color C.

Rows 58-65: Rep rows 42-49, using color B instead of color C. Tie off color B.

Rows 66-68: With color A, sk 1 st, dc in next 79 sts, ch 3, turn. End off.

To Make Tassels: You need 16 tassels per end. Cut 4 pieces of yarn 12 inches long. Thread 4 strands of yarn through the 1st dc of last row of sts. Tie strands in a square knot. Continue across both ends of rug, spacing tassels evenly.

Accent Pillow

To make the pillow, begin with 42 chs of color A. Dc in 2nd ch from hook and in each ch across. Ch 3, turn. Rows 2 and 3 are worked in the same manner (one dc in each dc across).

Rep the color pattern as established in the rug for the rest of the pillow (rows 4 through 19), changing yarn colors as necessary but not adding the solid stripes of color worked in the center of the rug.

Rep for other side. Sl st together and stuff.

We reversed the direction of the pattern on the pillow for added interest.

Open-work placemats *will add a touch of elegance to your next luncheon or dinner party. Design: Buff Bradley.*

Placemats for All Occasions

A simple combination of double crochet and chains creates the lacy look of these placemats. Either preshrink your twine or wash finished mats by hand in cold water.

Materials: Approximately 125 yards of household twine or size 24 macramé twine for each placemat J aluminum crochet hook (or hook to give proper gauge)

Gauge: 3 stitches = 1 inch; 1 row = 1 inch

Main Stitch: Double crochet

Size: 11½ by 16½ inches

Note: All dc are worked in back lps of sts in preceding row to created ridged effect, see page 72.

Ch 46.

Row 1: Dc in 2nd ch, dc in next 43 sts, ch 3, turn.

Row 2: Sk 1 st, dc in next 4 sts (all dc in back lp of sts), * ch 1, sk 1 st, dc in next st, rep from * 3x, dc in next 20 sts, ** ch 1, sk 1 st, dc in next st, rep from ** 3x; dc in next 4 sts, ch 3, turn.

Rows 3-4: Rep row 2.

Row 5: Sk 1 st, dc in next 43 sts, ch 3, turn.

Row 6: Sk 1 st, dc in next 12 sts; * ch 1, sk 1 st, dc in next st, rep from * 7x; dc in next 12 sts, ch 3, turn.

Rows 7-8: Rep row 6.

Row 9: Sk 1 st, dc in next 43 sts, ch 3, turn.

Rows 10-12: Rep row 2.

Row 13: Sk 1 st, dc in next 43 sts.

To Finish: Sl st all around outside border.

Crochet a rug and pillow *in earth tones to warm up your entryway or hearth. Design: Buff Bradley.*
Rug and Pillow: Instructions, page 55.

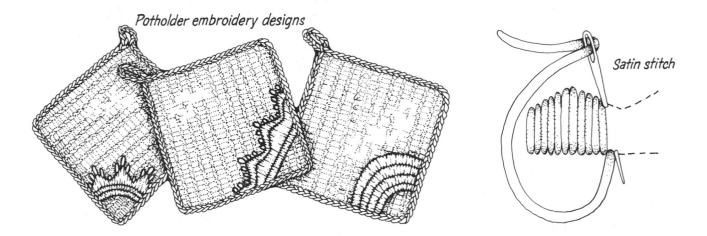

Potholder embroidery designs

Satin stitch

Potholders with Pizzazz

The afghan stitch (see pages 18-19) is a perfect choice for objects — such as potholders — which require a dense texture.

Once you've mastered these simple potholder squares, you can adapt the basic stitch to create designs of your own. We livened up our potholders by embroidering designs on them after they were blocked.

Materials: One 2-ounce skein 3-ply acrylic rug yarn of *each* color: color A (gold), color B (green), color C (navy)
Small amounts (a few yards) rug yarn or other washable bulky yarn for embroidery: red, gold, orange, light blue, green, lavender
J aluminum afghan hook (or hook to give proper gauge)
I aluminum crochet hook (or hook to give proper gauge)
Yarn needle

Gauge: 3 stitches = 1 inch; 5 rows = 2 inches

Main Stitch: Afghan stitch

Size: 7 by 7 inches

With J afghan hook and rug yarn, ch 22.

Row 1(a): Sk 1st ch from hook, pull up a lp in each ch across (keep all lps on hook).

Row 1(b): Yo, pull through 1st lp, * yo, pull through next 2 lps, rep from * across until 1 lp remains.

Row 2(a): Keeping all lps on hook, sk 1st vertical bar, pull up a lp under next vertical bar and under each vertical bar across.

Row 2(b): Work lps off as in row 1(b).

Brighten your kitchen *with perky potholders crocheted with washable rug yarn. Design: Lynne Morrall.*

Rows 3-18: Rep rows 2(a) and 2(b).

To Finish: Insert I hook in last lp of last row, sl st in each st around potholder, ch 1 at corners. When last corner is reached, ch 10, then sl st to 1st ch. End off. Weave yarn tails in with yarn needle. Block or steam flat. When dry, with yarn needle and using satin stitch, embroider designs onto potholders, following illustrations above.

Lazy·Day Hammock

Imagine yourself relaxing in this inviting hammock on a warm summer evening or on the first day of spring. It's comfortable and cool, and simple to make.

    The hammock is just a large rectangle of double crochet stitches and chains made of dacron or nylon cord. You may have to order the cord, since few shops have large quantities of either on hand. Try ship chandleries and craft supply shops.

Materials: Seven 1-pound rolls of white nylon or dacron seine twine, size 36. The hammock will require 6 rolls of the cord, or approximately 1,080 yards. The 7th roll of cord will be used to form the ends.
Two rings, 3 inches in diameter
Eight feet of 1-by-2-inch hardwood for the spreader
Epoxy or strong fabric glue
J aluminum crochet hook (or hook to give proper gauge)
Drill
Gauge: 1 double crochet and 3 chains = 1 inch; 1 row = 1 inch
Main Stitch: Double crochet
Size: 3 by 8 feet

Make a ch approximately 38 inches long (number of chs must be divisible by 4).
Row 1: Dc in the 5th ch from hook, * ch 2, sk 2 chs, dc in next 2 chs. Rep from * across, ending with 2 dc in the last 2 chs. Ch 3, turn.
Row 2: Dc in next stitch, * ch 2, sk 2 sts, dc in next 2 sts. Rep from * across, ending with dc in last st and dc in top of ch-3 from previous row. Ch 3, turn.
Row 3 to end: Rep row 2 until hammock is approximately 7 feet long. (If you are using nylon cord, keep in mind that it will stretch approximately a foot when in use.) When joining a new roll of cord, connect with a square knot and secure by reinforcing with glue, or melt the cord slightly to fuse the two.

Making the Spreader

1. Cut 2 pieces of hardwood 45 inches long. Sand smooth, and slightly round ends if desired.
2. You will need to make 9 evenly distributed holes. Determine center of each board for the 1st hole. Then measure 4¾ inches from center to left and to right. Using same 4¾-inch measure, make 3 *more* holes on each side of center.
3. Finish hardwood with stain and varnish or with paint (we used a walnut stain on ash).

To Form Strands

Attach last roll of cord to the end of the last row of the hammock with sl st. Sc in next st; then ch until approximately 54 inches long. End off, leaving about 4 feet extra cord for final wrapping. Continue across both ends, attaching a ch to every 4th set of 2 dc's.

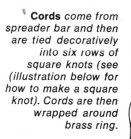

Cords come from spreader bar and then are tied decoratively into six rows of square knots (see illustration below for how to make a square knot). Cords are then wrapped around brass ring.

Detail of square knots

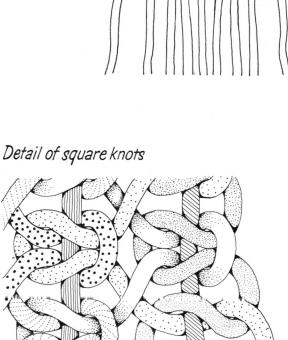

Enticing hammock *will lure you away from your chores on lazy summer days. Though the hammock is a big project to tackle, it's easy, for it's merely a large rectangle of repeats of chains and double crochets. You can use nylon or dacron cord; dacron is better, since it doesn't stretch. Design: Tina Kauffman.*

Finishing the Ends

1. Pull each 54-inch-long ch through the appropriate hole in the spreader and tie a secure overhand knot in the ch close to the outside of each hole.

2. Work one end at a time. With tension, pull all cords together at 30 inches above center of the spreader. Using 3 cords at a time, tie a row of square knots. Make sure all cords are evenly taut. For the next row of knots, crisscross cords as shown in drawing and tie another row of square knots with 3 cords each. Continue in the same manner until 6 rows have been completed.

3. Approximately 1 inch above square knots, make sure all chs stop and the plain cord continues. The last step will be done with lengths of cord rather than lengths of ch.

4. Attach ring as follows: with every other cord, loop through ring, tie to the next cord with square knot. With last cord, tie knot using the last three cords. Apply epoxy or strong glue so that these knots will not come loose. Cut 6 cords short. With the 3 long cords, wrap around and around the knotted area, looping through the ring a couple of times for strength. Tie securely and cut short. Apply glue to knots.

Youngsters and oldsters both love the cuddly feel of a hand-crocheted afghan.

Brighten up baby's world with a traditional ripple afghan made in a rainbow of untraditional colors.

Or decorate a corner of your couch or a loved one's lap with the traditional granny square afghan. A few unconventional touches were added just to keep you on your toes; note the half moon shapes on two sides and the bright accent rows of single and triple crochet in the border.

Rainbow Ripple Afghan

Made entirely of single crochet, this blanket has a unique ridged effect created by working in the back of the stitch of the previous row. The zigzag shape evolves after about the first five rows.

Acrylic knitting worsted is the most practical choice of yarn for a baby's afghan since it's so durable and is machine washable and dryable.

Materials: One 4-ounce skein of 4-ply acrylic knitting worsted in each of the following colors: color A (red), color B (orange), color C (yellow), color D (green), color E (blue), color F (purple)
J aluminum crochet hook (or hook to give proper gauge)
Yarn needle
Gauge: 4 stitches = 1 inch; 3 rows = 1 inch
Main Stitch: Single crochet
Size: 22 by 33 inches

Note: After row 1, you will always work in the *back* of the stitch of the previous row; therefore, you will always go through just one loop in the first step of each sc. (For more information on this technique, see page 72.)
With color A, ch 134, turn.
Row 1: 1 sc in 2nd ch from hook, 5 sc, * 3 sc in next ch, 7 sc, sk 2 chs, 7 sc, rep from * across to last 8 chs, 3 sc in next ch, sc in next 6 chs, leaving last ch unworked. Ch 1, turn.
Rows 2-10: Sk 1st st, 6 sc, * 3 sc in next st, 7 sc, sk 2 sts, 7 sc, continue from * across to last 8 sc, 3 sc in next st, 6 sc, leaving last st unworked. Ch 1, turn. At end of row 10, draw color B through last lp of last st (for other colors, change in this manner).
Rows 11-20: With color B, rep rows 2-10.
Rows 21-30: With color C, rep rows 2-10.
Rows 31-40: With color D, rep rows 2-10.

Rows 41-50: With color E, rep rows 2-10.
Rows 51-60: With color F, rep rows 2-10.
Rows 61-70: With color A, rep rows 2-10.
Rows 71-80: With color B, rep rows 2-10.
Rows 81-90: With color C, rep rows 2-10.
With yarn needle, weave in loose ends.

Granny Square Afghan

Although this afghan pattern is written for 9 colors, the number and combination of colors can be varied. This pattern lends itself to using up your scraps.

Materials: One 4-ounce skein 4-ply knitting worsted of each color, except color B, which calls for two 4-ounce skeins: color A (blue), color B (chartreuse), color C (lilac), color D (turquoise), color E (avocado green), color F (navy), color G (powder blue), color H (royal purple), color I (forest green), color J (royal blue), color K (light aqua)
G aluminum crochet hook (or hook to give proper gauge)
Yarn needle
Main Stitch: Double crochet
Gauge: 3 double crochet stitches = ½ inch, 1 row = 3 inches
Size: 45 inches square

With color A, ch 4, join with sl st to form ring.
Row 1: Ch 1, 8 sc in ring. Join with sl st to 1st sc.
Row 2: Draw lp to ½ inch, (yo and draw up ½-inch lp in same place as joining)3x, yo, draw through 7 lps on hook, ch 3, * in next sc (yo, draw up ½-inch lp 3x, yo and draw yarn through 7 lps, ch 3), rep from * 6x. Join with sl st.
Row 3: Sl st to ch-3 sp, ch 3, 2 dc, ch 2, 3 dc in same sp (corner made), * ch 1, 2 dc in next sp, ch 1, 3 dc in next sp, ch 2, 3 dc in same sp, rep from * 2x, ch 1, 2 dc in next sp, ch 1, join with sl st. End off. This should measure about 2 inches in diameter.
Row 4: Join color B in corner sp, ch 3, 2 dc, ch 2, 3 dc (corner made), * ch 1, 3 dc in next sp, rep from * 1x, ch 1, work corner. Work in the same manner around square, joining with a sl st. End off.
Row 5: Join color C in corner sp. Work as in row 4. There will be 3 groups of 3 dc in between corners. Join with sl st.
Row 6: Sl st across 3 dc to corner sp. Work as in row 4 (4 groups of 3 dc between corners). End off.
Row 7: Join color D in corner sp. Work as in row 4. End off.
Row 8: Join color E in corner sp. Work as in row 4.

Row 9: Sl st to corner, ch 3, 1 dc, ch 2, 2 dc in corner sp, * dc in each dc and sp of previous row, in corner sp 2 dc, ch 2, 2 dc, rep from * around. Join with sl st (112 dc around square).

Row 10: Sl st to corner sp, ch 3, 2 dc, ch 2, 3 dc (corner made), ch 1, sk 3 sts, 3 dc in next st, * ch 1, sk 2 sts, 3 dc in next st, rep from * across. Work evenly around square. (There will be 8 groups of 3 dc in between corners.) Join with sl st.

Row 11: Sl st to corner. Work as in row 4. End off.

Row 12: Join color F in corner sp, work as in row 4. End off.

Row 13: Join color B in corner sp, ch 3, 1 dc, ch 2, 2 dc (corner made), dc in each dc and sp of previous row, work the same around square (204 dc). Join with sl st.

Row 14: Sl st to corner. Work as in row 9.

Row 15: Sl st to corner. Work as in row 4. End off.

To Form Pyramids: on Sides 1 and 3

Row 16: Join color G in corner st. *Side 1:* in corner sp, ch 3, 2 dc, ch 2, 3 dc (corner made), * ch 1, 3 dc in next sp, rep from * 2x. Change to color B, rep from * 8x. Change back to color G, rep from * 3x. Ch 1. *Side 2:* work corner and along side as in previous rows, with no color change. *Side 3:* rep side 1. *Side 4:* rep side 2. Join with sl st.

Row 17: Sl st to corner. *Sides 1 and 3:* ch 3, 2 dc, ch 2, 3 dc (corner made), * ch 1, 3 dc in next sp, rep from * 3x. Change to color B, rep from * 7x. Change to color G, rep from * 4x. *Sides 2 and 4:* work the same as in previous rows with no color change. Join with sl st.

Row 18: Sl st to corner. *Sides 1 and 3:* ch 3, 2 dc, ch 2, 3 dc (corner made), * ch 1, 3 dc in next sp, rep from * 4x. Change to color B, rep from * 6x. Change to color G, rep from * 4x. *Sides 2 and 4:* work the same as in previous rows. Join with sl st.

Row 19: Sl st to corner. *Sides 1 and 3:* make corner as in row 16, * ch 1, 3 dc in next sp, rep from * 5x. Change to color B, rep from * 5x. Change to color G, rep from * 6x. *Sides 2 and 4:* work the same as previous rows, with no color change. Join with sl st.

Row 20: Sl st to corner. *Sides 1 and 3:* make corner as in row 16, * ch 1, 3 dc in next sp, rep from * 6x. Change to color B, rep from * 4x. Change to color G, rep from * 7x. *Sides 2 and 4:* work the same as in previous rows with no color change. Join with sl st. Pyramid is made.

Row 21: To make half circle at top of each pyramid, join color D in 5th dc from right edge of pyramid, ch 6, sk 2 dc, sl st to 8th dc from right edge of pyramid, ch 4 (counts as 1 tr), sk 4 sts, sl st to last dc in pyramid (left side). Turn.

Row 22: Make 11 tr into sp made by ch-6, sl st into 1st dc of pyramid edge. End off. (12 tr counting ch 4).

Note: Rep rows 21 and 22 on other side of afghan.

Row 23: Join color H in corner of row 20, ch 3, 2 dc, ch 2, 3 dc (corner made), * ch 1, 3 dc in next sp, continue from * across row (9 shells). At half circle, work as follows: 3 dc in sp next to half circle, sk 1st tr of half circle, sc in next 3 sts, 2 sc in next st, 1 sc in next st, 2 sc in next st, 1 sc in next 3 sts (11 sc), 3 dc in sp next to half circle.

Row 24: Sl st to corner, work corner and around square as in previous rows. At half circle, work 3 dc in sp (between 3 dc, ch) before half circle, sk 1st sc, sc in next 3 sts, 2 sc in next st, sc in next st, 2 sc in next st, sc in next 3 sts (11 sc), sk 1 sc, ch 1, 3 dc in sp.

Row 25: Sl st to corner, work corner and around square as in previous row (10 shells). At half circle, 3 dc in sp before half circle, sk 2 sc, sc in next 7 sts, 3 dc in sp next to half circle. End off.

Row 26: Join color I in corner sp, work around corner and square as in previous rows. At half circle, work 3 dc in sp before half circle, sk 1st sc, 2 sc in next st, 1 sc in next 3 sts, 2 sc in next sc (7 sc), 3 dc in sp after half circle.

Row 27: Sl st to corner, work around square and corner as in previous rows. At half circle, 3 dc in sp before half circle, sk 2 sts, sc in next 3 sc, 3 dc in sp after half circle.

Row 28: Sl st to corner, ch 4, 1 tr, ch 2, 2 tr (corner made). Tr in each dc and in ch between across row. Work the same around square. Join with sl st. End off. (Two sides will have 95 tr and two sides will have 103 tr.)

Row 29: Join color J in corner sp, ch 3, 1 dc, ch 2, 2 dc (corner made), * ch 1, sk st, 1 dc in next st across row. Continue around square in same manner. Join with sl st.

Row 30: Sl st to corner, ch 3, 2 dc, ch 2, 3 dc (corner made). 2 dc in each sp in previous row. Work in same manner around square. Join with sl st.

Row 31: Sl st to corner, ch 3, 2 dc, ch 2, 3 dc (corner made). 1 dc in each st across row. Work in same manner around square. Join with sl st. End off.

Row 32: Join color I in corner sp, ch 2, 2 sc in corner, sc in each st across row. Work in same manner around square (corners made with 3 sc). Join with sl st. End off.

Row 33: Join color J at corner sc, ch 2, 2 sc in joining place. Sc in each st across row. Work in same manner around square (corners made with 3 sc). Join with sl st. End off.

Row 34: Join color C and rep row 33. End off.

Row 35: Join color J and rep row 33. End off.

Row 36: Join color B in corner sp. Ch 3, 2 dc, ch 2, 3 dc (corner made), * ch 1, sk 3 sts, 3 dc in next st, rep from * across row, continue as in previous rows around square. Join with sl st.

Rows 37-39: Sl st to corner, ch 3, 2 dc, ch 2, 3 dc (corner made), * ch 1, 3 dc in next sp, rep from * across row, work in same manner around square. Join with sl st.

Row 40: Sl st to corner, ch 2, 2 sc in corner, sc in each dc and in each ch across row. Work in same manner around square (corners made with 3 sc). Join with sl st. End off.

Row 41: Join color K at corner sc, ch 2, 2 sc in joining place, sc in each st across row. Work in same manner around square (corners made with 3 sc). Join with sl st. End off.

Row 42: Join color B, ch 2, rep row 41. End off.

Choose **machine washable yarn** *for baby's first afghan, such as a bright rainbow of acrylic knitting worsted. This one has been machine washed and dried over 50 times. Design: Lynne Morrall. Rainbow Ripple Afghan: Instructions, page 60.*

Occasional bright stripes *of color and a pair of half-moon shapes add pizzazz to a traditional granny square afghan. Use up your leftover yarn scraps for a very personal color scheme. Design: Karen Cummings. Granny Square Afghan: Instructions begin on page 60.*

Elegant Afghan

(Color photo on page 64)

First you crochet the center square; then
you work the border around the square.
Finally, you add the side panels.

Materials: 4-ply acrylic knitting worsted: three 4-ounce
skeins *each* of color A (red), color B (burgundy), col-
or C (orange); two 4-ounce skeins color D (pink);
one 2-ounce skein color E (bright blue)
H aluminum crochet hook (or hook to give proper
gauge)
Gauge: 4 stitches = 1 inch; 4 rows = 1 inch
Main Stitch: Single crochet
Size: 45 by 50 inches

Central Square

With color A, ch 82.

Row 1: Sc in 3rd ch from hook and in each ch across.
Note: (ch 2 and turn at the end of *each* row).

Rows 2-5: Sc in each st across.

Row 6: Add color B and carry yarn inside sts until
used (work the same throughout afghan, carrying colors used in row along entire row inside sts, see page
30). With color A, sc in 10 sts; with color B, sc in next
20 sts; with color A, sc in next 20 sts; with color B, sc
in next 20 sts; with color A, sc in next 10 sts.

Row 7: With color A, sc in 11 sts; with color B, sc in
next 18 sts; with color A, sc in next 22 sts; with color
B, sc in next 18 sts; with color A, sc in next 11 sts.

Row 8: With color A, sc in 12 sts; with color B, sc in
next 16 sts; with color A, sc in next 24 sts; with color
B, sc in next 16 sts; with color A, sc in next 12 sts.

Row 9: With color A, sc in 13 sts; with color B, sc in
next 14 sts; with color A, sc in next 26 sts; with color
B, sc in next 14 sts; with color A, sc in next 13 sts.

Row 10: With color A, sc in 14 sts; with color B, sc in
next 12 sts; with color A, sc in next 28 sts; with color
B, sc in next 12 sts; with color A, sc in next 14 sts.

Row 11: With color A, sc in 15 sts; with color B, sc in
next 10 sts; with color A, sc in next 30 sts; with color
B, sc in next 10 sts; with color A, sc in next 15 sts.

Row 12: With color A (carry colors B and C), sc in 5
sts; with color B, sc in next st; with color A, sc in next
10 sts; with color B, sc in next 8 sts; with color A, sc
in next 10 sts; with color C, sc in next st; with color
A, sc in next 10 sts; with color C, sc in next st; with
color A, sc in next 10 sts; with color B, sc in next 8 sts;
with color A, sc in next 10 sts; with color B, sc in next
st; with color A, sc in next 5 sts.

Row 13: With color A, sc in 5 sts; with color B, sc in
next 2 sts; with color A, sc in next 10 sts; with color
B, sc in next 6 sts; with color A, sc in next 10 sts; with
color C, sc in next 2 sts; with color A, sc in next 10
sts; with color C, sc in next 2 sts; with color A, sc in
next 10 sts; with color B, sc in next 6 sts; with color A,
sc in next 10 sts; with color B, sc in next 2 sts; with
color A, sc in next 5 sts.

Row 14: With color A, sc in 5 sts; with color B, sc in
next 3 sts; with color A, sc in next 10 sts; with color
B, sc in next 4 sts; with color A, sc in next 10 sts; with
color C, sc in next 3 sts; with color A, sc in next 10
sts; with color C, sc in next 3 sts; with color A, sc in
next 10 sts; with color B, sc in next 4 sts; with color
A, sc in next 10 sts; with color B, sc in next 3 sts; with
color A, sc in next 5 sts.

Row 15: With color A, sc in 5 sts; with color B, sc in
next 4 sts; with color A, sc in next 10 sts; with color
B, sc in next 2 sts; with color A, sc in next 10 sts; with
color C, sc in next 4 sts; with color A, sc in next 10
sts; with color C, sc in next 4 sts; with color A, sc in
next 10 sts; with color B, sc in next 2 sts; with color
A, sc in next 10 sts; with color B, sc in next 4 sts;
with color A, sc in next 5 sts.

Row 16: With color A, sc in 5 sts; with color B, sc in
next 5 sts; with color A, sc in next 20 sts; with color C,
sc in next 5 sts; with color A, sc in next 10 sts; with
color C, sc in next 5 sts; with color A, sc in next 20
sts; with color B, sc in next 5 sts; with color A, sc in
next 5 sts.

Row 17: With color A, sc in 5 sts; with color B, sc in
next 6 sts; with color A, sc in next 18 sts; with color
C, sc in next 6 sts; with color A, sc in next 10 sts; with
color C, sc in next 6 sts; with color A, sc in next 18
sts; with color B, sc in next 6 sts; with color A, sc in
next 5 sts.

Row 18: With color A, sc in 5 sts; with color B, sc in
next 7 sts; with color A, sc in next 16 sts; with color
C, sc in next 7 sts; with color A, sc in next 10 sts; with
color C, sc in next 7 sts; with color A, sc in next 16
sts; with color B, sc in next 7 sts; with color A, sc in
next 5 sts.

Row 19: With color A, sc in 5 sts; with color B, sc in
next 8 sts; with color A, sc in next 14 sts; with color
C, sc in next 8 sts; with color A, sc in next 10 sts; with
color C, sc in next 8 sts; with color A, sc in next 14
sts; with color B, sc in next 8 sts; with color A, sc in
next 5 sts.

Row 20: With color A, sc in 5 sts; with color B, sc in
next 9 sts; with color A, sc in next 12 sts; with color C,
sc in next 9 sts; with color A, sc in next 10 sts; with
color C, sc in next 9 sts; with color A, sc in next 12
sts; with color B, sc in next 9 sts; with color A, sc in
next 5 sts.

Row 21: With color A, sc in 5 sts; with color B, sc in
next 10 sts; with color A, sc in next 10 sts; with color
C, sc in next 10 sts; with color A, sc in next 10 sts; with
color C, sc in next 10 sts; with color A, sc in next 10
sts; with color B, sc in next 10 sts; with color A, sc in
next 5 sts.

Rows 22-26: Rep rows 20-16 respectively.

Row 27: With color A, sc in 5 sts; with color B, sc in
next 4 sts; with color A, sc in next 10 sts; with color
C, sc in next 2 sts; with color A, sc in next 10 sts; with
color C, sc in next 4 sts; with color A, sc in next 10
sts; with color C, sc in next 4 sts; with color A, sc in
next 10 sts; with color C, sc in next 2 sts; with color
A, sc in next 10 sts; with color B, sc in next 4 sts; with
color A, sc in next 5 sts.

Row 28: With color A, sc in 5 sts; with color B, sc in
next 3 sts; with color A, sc in next 10 sts; with color

(Continued on next page)

C, sc in next 4 sts; with color A, sc in next 10 sts; with color C, sc in next 3 sts; with color A, sc in next 10 sts; with color C, sc in next 3 sts; with color A, sc in next 10 sts; with color C, sc in next 4 sts; with color A, sc in next 10 sts; with color B, sc in next 3 sts; with color A, sc in next 5 sts.

Row 29: With color A, sc in 5 sts; with color B, sc in next 2 sts; with color A, sc in next 10 sts; with color C, sc in next 6 sts; with color A, sc in next 10 sts; with color C, sc in next 2 sts; with color A, sc in next 10 sts; with color C, sc in next 2 sts; with color A, sc in next 10 sts; with color C, sc in next 6 sts; with color A, sc in next 10 sts; with color B, sc in next 2 sts; with color A, sc in next 5 sts.

Row 30: With color A, sc in 5 sts; with color B, sc in next st; with color A, sc in next 10 sts; wtih color C, sc in next 8 sts; with color A, sc in next 10 sts; with color C, sc in next st; with color A, sc in next 10 sts; with color C, sc in next st; with color A, sc in next 10 sts; with color C, sc in next 8 sts; with color A, sc in next 10 sts; with color B, sc in next st; with color A, sc in next 5 sts.

Row 31: With color A, sc in 15 sts; with color C, sc in next 10 sts; with color A, sc in next 30 sts; with color C, sc in next 10 sts; with color A, sc in next 15 sts.

Row 32: With color A, sc in 14 sts; with color C, sc in next 12 sts; with color A, sc in 28 sts; with color C, sc in next 12 sts; with color A, sc in next 14 sts.

Row 33: With color A, sc in 13 sts; with color C, sc in next 14 sts; with color A, sc in next 26 sts; with color C, sc in next 14 sts; with color A, sc in next 13 sts.

Row 34: With color A, sc in 12 sts; with color C, sc in next 16 sts; with color A, sc in next 24 sts; with color C, sc in next 16 sts; with color A, sc in next 12 sts.

Row 35: With color A, sc in 11 sts; with color C, sc in next 18 sts; with color A, sc in next 22 sts; with color C, sc in next 18 sts; with color A, sc in next 11 sts.

Row 36: With color A, sc in 10 sts; with color C, sc in next 20 sts; with color A, sc in next 20 sts; with color C, sc in next 20 sts; with color A, sc in next 10 sts.

Rows 37-46: With color A, work 1 sc in each sc across (continue carrying colors B and C within sts to keep weight the same).

Row 47: Reverse pattern, starting with row 36 and working back to row 1; end off.

Working Around Square

Each row is worked on alternate side of afghan. At the end of each row, join with sl st, end off, and turn.

Row 1: Join color A at corner of row 1 of square, ch 2, sc in each st across row, making 3 sc in corner st; sc along side, making 1 sc in end of each row; continue in same manner around square.

Row 2: Join color E at corner, sc in each st around square, making 3 sc in corner sts.

Rows 3-7: With color B, rep row 2.

Row 8: *Side 1:* join color C at corner, ch 2, 2 sc in corner sp (keeping color B inside), sc in next 4 sts; * with color B, sc in next 20 sts; with color C, sc in next 2 sts; rep from * 2x; with color B, sc in next 20 sts; with color C, sc in next 4 sts. *Side 2:* with color C,

Curl up on the couch *with kitty and afghan, or let both decorate the house. Keeping the cat perched on the table is a problem, but the afghan can be tacked to a board and hung on the wall. Instructions begin on page 63. Design: Karen Cummings.*

3 sc in corner and 1 sc in each st along side. *Side 3:* rep pat of side 1. *Side 4:* rep pat of side 2.

Row 9: *Side 1:* join color C at corner, ch 2, 2 sc in corner sp, sc in next 6 sts, * with color B, sc in next 18 sts; with color C, sc in next 4 sts; rep from * 2x; with color B, sc in next 18 sts; with color C, sc in next 6 sts. *Side 2:* with color C, 3 sc in corner and 1 sc in each st along side. *Side 3:* rep side 1. *Side 4:* rep side 2.

Note: On rows 10-26, work side 1 as instructed. For side 3, rep side 1. For sides 2 and 4, rep as in row 9.

Row 10: *Side 1:* join color C at corner, ch 2, 2 sc in corner sp, sc in 8 sts; * with color B, sc in next 16 sts; with color C, sc in next 6 sts; rep from * 2x; with color B, sc in next 16 sts; with C, sc in next 8 sts.

Row 11: *Side 1:* join color C at corner, ch 2, 2 sc in corner sp, sc in next 10 sts; * with color B, sc in next 14 sts; with color C, sc in next 8 sts; rep from * 2x; with color B, sc in next 14 sts; with color C, sc in next 10 sts.

Row 12: *Side 1:* join color C at corner, ch 2, 2 sc in corner sp, sc in next 12 sts; * with color B, sc in next 12 sts; with color C, sc in next 4 sts; with color D, sc in next 2 sts; with color C, sc in next 4 sts; rep from * 2x; with color B, sc in next 12 sts; with color C, sc in next 12 sts.

Row 13: *Side 1:* join color C at corner, ch 2, 2 sc in corner sp, sc in next 14 sts; * with color B, sc in next 10 sts; with color C, sc in next 4 sts; with color D, sc in next 4 sts; with color C, sc in next 4 sts; rep from * 2x; with B, sc in next 10 sts; with C, sc in next 14 sts.

Row 14: *Side 1:* join color C at corner, ch 2, 2 sc in corner sp, sc in next 16 sts; * with color B, sc in next 8 sts; with color C, sc in next 4 sts; with color D, sc in next 6 sts; with color C, sc in next 4 sts; rep from * 2x; with B, sc in next 8 sts; with C, sc in next 16 sts.

Row 15: *Side 1:* join color C at corner, ch 2, 2 sc in corner sp, sc in next 18 sts; * with color B, sc in next 6 sts; with color C, sc in next 4 sts; with color D, sc in next 8 sts; with color C, sc in next 4 sts; rep from * 2x; with B, sc in next 6 sts; with C, sc in next 18 sts.

Row 16: *Side 1:* join color C at corner, ch 2, 2 sc in corner sp, sc in next 20 sts; * with color B, sc in next 4 sts; with color C, sc in next 4 sts; with color D, sc in next 4 sts; with color B, sc in next 2 sts; with color D, sc in next 4 sts; with color C, sc in next 4 sts; rep from * 2x; with B, sc in next 4 sts; with C, sc in next 20 sts.

Row 17: *Side 1:* join color C at corner, ch 2, 2 sc in corner sp, sc in next 22 sts; * with color B, sc in next 2 sts; with color C, sc in next 4 sts; with color D, sc in next 4 sts; with color B, sc in next 4 sts; with color D, sc in next 4 sts; with color C, sc in next 4 sts; rep from * 2x; with B, sc in next 2 sts; with C, sc in next 22 sts.

Row 18: *Side 1:* join color C at corner, ch 2, 2 sc in corner sp, sc in next 22 sts; * with color B, sc in next 4 sts; with color C, sc in next 4 sts; with color D, sc in next 4 sts; with color B, sc in next 2 sts; with color D, sc in next 4 sts; with color C, sc in next 4 sts; rep from * 2x; with B, sc in next 4 sts; with C, sc in next 22 sts.

Row 19: *Side 1:* join color C at corner, ch 2, 2 sc in corner sp, sc in next 22 sts; * with color B, sc in next 6 sts; with color C, sc in next 4 sts; with color D, sc in next 8 sts; with color C, sc in next 4 sts; rep from * 2x; with B, sc in next 6 sts; with C, sc in next 22 sts.

Row 20: *Side 1:* join color C at corner, ch 2, 2 sc in corner sp, sc in next 22 sts; * with color B, sc in next 8 sts; with color C, sc in next 4 sts; with color D, sc in next 6 sts; with color C, sc in next 4 sts; rep from * 2x; with B, sc in next 8 sts; with C, sc in next 22 sts.

Row 21: *Side 1:* join color C at corner, ch 2, 2 sc in corner sp, sc in next 22 sts; * with color B, sc in next 10 sts; with color C, sc in next 4 sts; with color D, sc in next 4 sts; with color C, sc in next 4 sts; rep from * 2x; with B, sc in next 10 sts; with C, sc in next 22 sts.

Row 22: *Side 1:* join color C at corner, ch 2, 2 sc in corner sp, sc in next 22 sts; * with color B, sc in next 12 sts; with color C, sc in next 4 sts; with color D, sc in next 2 sts; with color C, sc in next 4 sts; rep from * 2x; with B, sc in next 12 sts; with C, sc in next 22 sts.

Row 23: *Side 1:* join color C at corner, ch 2, 2 sc in corner sp, sc in next 22 sts; * with color B, sc in next 14 sts; with color C, sc in next 8 sts; rep from * 2x; with color B, sc in next 14 sts; with color C, sc in next 22 sts.

Row 24: *Side 1:* join color C at corner, ch 2, 2 sc in corner sp, sc in next 22 sts; * with color B, sc in next 16 sts; with color C, sc in next 6 sts; rep from *2x; with color B, sc in next 16 sts; with C, sc in next 22 sts.

Row 25: *Side 1:* join color C at corner, ch 2, 2 sc in corner sp, sc in next 22 sts; * with color B, sc in next 18 sts; with color C, sc in next 4 sts; rep from * 2x; with color B, sc in next 18 sts; with color C, sc in next 22 sts.

Row 26: *Side 1:* join color C at corner, ch 2, 2 sc in corner sp, sc in next 22 sts; * with color B, sc in next 20 sts; with color C, sc in next 2 sts; rep from * 2x; with color B, sc in next 20 sts; with color C, sc in next 22 sts.

Rows 27-31: Join color B at corner, sc in each st around, 3 sc in corner sts.

Row 32: Join color E, rep row 27.

Rows 33-37: Join color A, rep row 27. End off.

End Motifs: on sides 2 and 4

Row 1: Join color A at corner (carrying B inside), ch 2, sc in 12 sts; * with color C, sc in next 20 sts; with color A, sc in next 2 sts; rep from * 4x; with color C, sc in next 20 sts; with color A, sc in next 13 sts (to end of row); ch 2, turn.

Row 2: With color A, sc in next 13 sts; * with color C, sc in next 18 sts; with color A, sc in next 4 sts; rep from * 4x; with color C, sc in next 18 sts; with color A, sc in next 14 sts; ch 2, turn.

Row 3: With color A, sc in next 14 sts; * with color C, sc in next 16 sts; with color A, sc in next 6 sts; rep from * 4x; with color C, sc in next 16 sts; with color A, sc in next 15 sts; ch 2, turn.

Row 4: With color A, sc in next 15 sts; * with color C, sc in next 14 sts; with color A, sc in next 8 sts; rep from * 4x; with color C, sc in next 14 sts; with color A, sc in next 16 sts; ch 2, turn.

Row 5: With color A, sc in next 16 sts; * with color C, sc in next 12 sts; with color A, sc in next 10 sts; rep from * 4x; with color C, sc in next 12 sts; with color A, sc in next 17 sts; ch 2, turn.

Row 6: With color A, sc in next 17 sts; * with color C, sc in next 10 sts; with color A, sc in next 12 sts; rep from * 4x; with color C, sc in next 10 sts; with color A, sc in next 18 sts; ch 2, turn.

Row 7: With color A, sc in next 18 sts; * with color C, sc in next 8 sts; with color A, sc in next 14 sts; rep from * 4x; with color C, sc in next 8 sts; with color A, sc in next 19 sts; ch 2, turn.

Row 8: With color A, sc in next 19 sts; * with color C, sc in next 6 sts; with color A, sc in next 16 sts; rep from * 4x; with color C, sc in next 6 sts; with color A, sc in next 20 sts; ch 2, turn.

Row 9: With color A, sc in next 20 sts; * with color C, sc in next 4 sts; with color A, sc in next 18 sts; rep from * 4x; with color C, sc in next 4 sts; with color A, sc in next 21 sts; ch 2, turn.

Row 10: With color A, sc in next 21 sts; * with color C, sc in next 2 sts; with color A, sc in next 20 sts; rep from * 4x; with color C, sc in next 2 sts; with color A, sc in next 22 sts, ch 2, turn.

Rows 11-15: With color A, sc across row, ch 2, turn. End off at end of row 15.

To Finish: Work 1 row of sc with color E around outer edge of entire afghan. End off.

Slings & Things

Even dedicated macramé devotees will be converted to crochet when they see these plant slings and covers. House plants will love them and so will you because they work up so quickly. Large crochet hooks are used with heavy macramé twine, so you may wish to wear cotton gloves when working with the rough yarns.

Triple Spiral

After making a long chain for each strand of this unusual hanger, you simply double crochet down the chain. The spiral forms when you put the two double crochets in each chain.

Materials: Approximately 100 yards of 3-ply jute
H aluminum crochet hook (or hook to give proper gauge)
Gauge: 5 double crochet = 2 inches
Main Stitch: Double crochet
Size: Approximately 3 feet long (including tassel)

To form each strand (make three)
Ch 75. Turn, dc in 3rd ch from hook and in each ch for the next 15 sts, 2 dc in each ch for the next 39 sts, 1 dc in each ch for the last 18 sts. End off. (Check gauge periodically to make sure it is consistent, since all three strands must be exactly the same length for the finished piece to hang correctly.)

Top: Sl st through the ch-3 (finished) end of each strand, pulling jute back through all 3 strands. Ch 14, turn, dc in 7th ch from hook. Dc in each ch and fasten with sl st into top of strands. End off. Tie ends securely with square knot (for square knot see page 58).

Bottom: Tie off ends of each strand with square knot, making sure all 3 strands have an equal number of twists. Sl st through all ends as for top, and tie off securely with a square knot.

Tassel: Wrap jute around 6¼-inch square of cardboard 25 times. Tie one end and cut the other. Then wrap the tassel 1½ inches down from the top with matching jute. Tie with a square knot to bottom of hanger.

Granny Planter

Five macramé twine granny squares slip stitched together make this lacy plant cover. Crocheting with twine takes a bit more patience than working with yarn since twine is stiffer and less resilient than yarn.

Macrame look-alikes are easy-to-make crocheted plant hangers. Designs: Knobby collar (upper left), triple spiral hanger (upper right), jute plant cosy (lower left), Tina Kauffman; granny planter (lower right), Jane Hummert.

Materials: 1 ball (about 250 yards) of 3-ply cotton macramé twine, size 24
J aluminum crochet hook (or hook to give proper gauge)
Gauge: Complete square measures 5½ by 5½ inches
Main Stitch: Double crochet
Size: Fits 6-inch plant pot

To make each granny square (you will need 5)
Ch 6, join with sl st to form ring.
Row 1: Ch 3, 2 dc in ring, ch 3, * 3 dc in ring, ch 3, rep from * twice. Join with sl st to top of 1st ch-3.
Row 2: Ch 3, turn, 2 dc in ch-3 sp of previous row (not 1st ch-3). Ch 3, 3 dc in *same* ch-3 sp, ch 1 (this forms the corner). * 3 dc, ch 3, 3 dc, ch 1 in next ch-3 sp. Rep from * in the next 2 sps. Join with sl st to top of 1st ch-3 of row 2.
Row 3: Ch 3, 2 dc, ch 1 in middle sp. * 3 dc, ch 3, 3 dc, ch 1 in corner, 3 dc, ch 1 in middle sp. Rep from * 2 more times, 3 dc, ch 3, 3 dc, ch 1 in last corner. To finish, sl st to top of 1st ch-3 of row 3. End off.

To Finish: Using 1 square as a base and the other 4 for sides, sl st squares together on all edges. Sc around top of planter. *To make straps,* start in one corner of planter and make a ch 30 inches long; sl st to opposite corner. Ch 1, turn, and sl st in each ch across to original corner. Rep for other strap.

Knobby Collar

This plant collar, made quickly of a simple combination of single crochets and chains, fits snugly under the rim of a standard clay flower pot.

Materials: Approximately 100 yards of 3-ply jute
H aluminum crochet hook (or hook to give proper gauge)
Yarn needle
Gauge: 7 stitches = 3 inches; 3 rows = 1½ inches
Size: Fits standard 8-inch clay plant pot
Main Stitch: Single crochet

To Form Band, ch 7.
Row 1: 1 sc in 2nd ch from hook and in each ch across. Ch 1, turn.
Row 2: 1 sc in each sc, ch 4, turn.
Row 3: 1 tr in back lp (see page 72) of 2nd sc and in back of each sc across. Ch 1, turn.
Row 4: * 1 sc in back lp of next st and in back lp of corresponding st on row below; rep from * to end. Ch 1, turn.
Row 5: 1 sc in each sc. Ch 1, turn. Rep rows 2-5 until desired length. (In determining proper length, be sure fit is *very snug,* especially under lip of pot, since jute stretches quite a bit.) End with a row 4. With right sides together, sl st ends together. End off. Weave ends into work with yarn needle.

To Make Hangers (make two): With sl st, attach new strand of yarn to the top of one of the "bumps." Make a ch 48 inches long and sl st to top of bump on opposite side of band; ch 1, turn. Sc in each ch to end. Attach to original bump. End off. Weave ends in.

With hangers crossing each other at top, come down about 2 inches and securely fasten them together with an overhand knot (see illustration below). Finish by wrapping a length of jute tightly around fastened area.

Overhand Knot

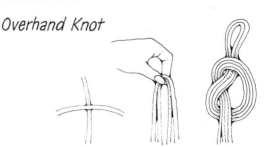

Plant Cosy

What do a cloche hat and a planter cover have in common? Both are made by the same basic method. You start with a chain, form a ring, and then work out in a circle. Once you've reached the proper diameter, you work up (or, for the hat, down) in a spiral.

Materials: Approximately 100 yards of 3-ply jute or rug yarn
K aluminum crochet hook (or hook to give proper gauge)
Gauge: 3 stitches = 1 inch; 1 row = 1 inch
Main Stitch: Double crochet
Size: 7 inches high by 7 inches in diameter

Beginning at center bottom, ch 4, join to 1st ch with sl st to form a ring.
Rnd 1: Ch 3, 11 dc in ring, join with sl st to top of ch-3 (ch 3 will count as 1st dc).
Rnd 2: Ch 3, dc in 1st st, 2 dc in each st around (24 sts). Join with sl st.
Rnd 3: Ch 3, dc in 1st st, 2 dc in each st around (48 sts). Join with sl st. If diameter is not large enough, rep rnd 3 until correct size. Number of sts in this rnd must be a multiple of 3, and this number will be the same in each rnd from now on.
Rnd 4: Ch 1. With hook coming from back to front, sc in the back lp of each st around. Join with sl st.
Rnd 5: Ch 3, dc in each st around (48 sts). Join with sl st.
Rnd 6: Ch 5, * sk 2 sts, dc in next st, ch 2. Rep from * around. Join to 3rd ch.
Rnds 7-8: Rep rnds 5 and 6.
Rnds 9-10: Rep rnd 5. End off and weave in end. (If cover is not tall enough, rep rnds 5 and 6 until desired height. End with a rnd 5.)

Dash around town *with this flashy backpack made of washable acrylic yarn. Design: Buff Bradley.*

Flashy Backpack

Pack a sandwich and a soda or brunch and a bikini in this backpack and you're ready to go.

You crochet the bag in one long piece, and then fold it in half and sew the side seams. The color-coordinated straps are crocheted separately, then sewn on.

Materials: 4-ply acrylic or wool knitting worsted: two 4-ounce skeins color A (gray), one 2-ounce skein *each* color B (red), color C (orange), color D (purple)
½ yard of 45-inch-wide dark gray cotton fabric
Yarn needle
F aluminum crochet hook (or hook to give proper gauge)
Button

Gauge: 4 stitches = 2 inches; 2 rows = 1 inch

Main Stitch: Double crochet

Note: All dc are worked in back lps of sts in preceding row to created ridged effect, see page 72.
With color A, ch 57.

Row 1: Dc in 2nd ch, dc in next 54 sts, ch 3, turn.

Row 2: Sk 1 st, dc in next 54 sts, ch 3, turn.

Rows 3-5: Rep row 2.

Row 6: Sk 1 st, dc in next 26 sts; with color B, dc in next st; with color A, dc in next 27 sts, ch 3, turn.

Row 7: Sk 1 st, dc in next 25 sts; with color B, dc in next 3 sts; with color A, dc in next 26 sts, ch 3, turn.

Row 8: Sk 1 st, dc in next 24 sts; with color B, dc in next 2 sts; with color C, dc in next st; with color B, dc in next 2 sts; with color A, dc in next 25 sts, ch 3, turn.

Row 9: Sk 1 st, dc in next 22 sts; with color B, dc in next 3 sts; with color C, dc in next 3 sts; with color B, dc in next 3 sts; with color A, dc in next 23 sts; with color B, ch 3, turn.

Row 10: Sk 1 st, dc in next 24 sts; with color C, dc in next 2 sts; with color D, dc in next st; with color C, dc in next 2 sts; with color B, dc in next 25 sts, ch 3, turn.

Row 11: Sk 1 st, dc in next 23 sts; with color C, dc in next 2 sts; with color D, dc in next 3 sts; with color C, dc in next 2 sts; with color B, dc in next 24 sts; with color C, ch 3, turn.

Row 12: Sk 1 dc, dc in next 24 sts; with color D, dc in next 2 sts; with color A, dc in next st; with color D, dc in next 2 sts; with color C, dc in next 25 sts, ch 3, turn.

Row 13: Sk 1 st, dc in next 23 sts; with color D, dc in next 2 sts; with color A, dc in next 3 sts; with color D, dc in next 2 sts; with color C, dc in next 24 sts; with color D, ch 3, turn.

Row 14: Sk 1 st; with color D, dc in next 24 sts; with color A, dc in next 5 sts; with color D, dc in next 25 sts, ch 3, turn.

Row 15: Sk 1 st; with color D, dc in next 23 sts; with color A, dc in next 7 sts; with color D, dc in next 24 sts; with color A, ch 3, turn.

Row 16: Sk 1 st, dc in next 54 sts, ch 3, turn.

Rows 17-44: Rep row 16. End off.

Straps (Make two)
With color A, ch 18.

Row 1: Dc in 2nd ch, dc in next 15 sts, ch 3, turn.

Row 2: Sk 1 st, dc in next 15 sts, ch 3, turn.

Rows 3-10: Rep row 2; with color B, ch 3, turn.

Rows 11-12: Sk 1 dc, dc in next 15 sts; with color C, ch 3, turn.

Rows 13-14: Sk 1 st, dc in next 15 sts; with color D, ch 3, turn.

Rows 15-16: Sk 1 st, dc in next 15 sts; with color A, ch 3, turn.

Rows 17-26: Rep row 2. End off.

To Finish: Cut piece of lining fabric the same width but about 2 inches shorter than bag. Lay bag out flat, wrong side facing up. Place fabric over bag, with about 1 inch of bag showing at each end. Sew fabric to bag at top and bottom, using a yarn needle and color A. Fold bag in half, lining side out. Sew sides together, about ½ inch in from the edges. Turn right side out.

Straps: Cut two strips of fabric the same length as the straps but about half as wide. Place straps on table, wrong side facing up. Center the strips of lining on the straps and fold edges of straps over lining to center. Sew straps together, using yarn needle and color A; then sew straps to bag.

Loop for button. With color A, ch 32. Sc in 2nd ch and in each ch across, finish off. Attach loop to back of bag with yarn needle and color A. Be sure to sew through lining of bag. Select button to fit button loop and sew to bag.

Cover Your Racket

Made in two identical and separate pieces (front and back), the racket cover is worked from the top down. Ours fits a traditionally shaped racket, but if you want a different shape, trace around the racket, add ½ inch, then increase or decrease to fit the shape.

Materials: 1 skein acrylic 4-ply knitting worsted of *each* color: color A (white), color B (navy blue), color C (red)
E aluminum crochet hook (or hook to give proper gauge)
9-inch zipper (white)
Gauge: 9 stitches = 2 inches; 5 rows = 2 inches
Main Stitch: Single crochet

Make Two Pieces (front and back)
With color A, ch 13.
Row 1: * Sc in 2nd ch from hook, sc in next 2 chs, 2 sc in next ch, rep from * to end of row (ending with 2 sc in last ch). 2 dc in last ch (same as last 2 sc), ch 1, turn.
Row 2: 2 sc in 1st st, * sc in next 3 chs, 2 sc in next ch, rep from * to end of row, ending with 2 sc in the last st. 2 dc in same st, ch 1, turn.
Row 3: 2 dc in 1st st, sc across row, ending with 2 dc in last st, ch 1, turn.
Rows 4-9: Rep row 3.
Row 10: Dc in 1st st, sc across row, ending with sc and dc in last st, ch 1, turn.
Rows 11-13: Rep row 10.
Row 14: Sc across row, ch 1, turn.
Row 15: Sc across row. Tie on color B, ch 1, turn.
Row 16: 2 sc in 1st st, sc across row, ending with 2 sc in last st, ch 1, turn.
Row 17: Sc across row, ch 1, turn.
Row 18: 2 sc in 1st st, sc across row, ending with 2 sc in last st, ch 1, turn.
Rows 19-23: Rep rows 17 and 18 (you end with a row 17). Tie on color A, ch 1, turn.
Row 24: Rep row 18.
Rows 25-30: Rep row 17.
Row 31: Sc across row, dec'ing 1 st at beginning and end of row. Tie on color C, ch 1, turn.
Row 32: Sc across row, ch 1, turn.
Rows 33-34: Sc across row, ch 1, turn.
Row 35: Sc across row, dec'ing 1 st at beginning and end of row, ch 1, turn.
Row 36: Sc across row, ch 1, turn.
Row 37: Rep row 35.
Row 38: Rep row 36.
Row 39: Rep row 35. Tie on color A, ch 1, turn.

Row 40: Sc across row, ch 1, turn.
Row 41: Rep row 35.
Rows 42-43: Rep row 36.
Rows 44-48: Rep rows 35 and 36 (you end with a row 35).
Row 49: Rep row 35.

Zip up your game *in patriotic style with a zippered racket cover of single crochet. Design: Tina Kauffman.*

Row 50: Rep row 36.
Rows 51-52: Rep row 35.
Row 53: Rep row 36.
Rows 54-60: Rep row 35.
Row 61: Rep row 36.
Row 62: Rep row 35.
Rows 63-65: Rep row 36. End off. Weave in ends.

To Finish: With right sides together, sl st the two pieces together near the edges. When you come to the color changes, tie off white and add the appropriate color. Stop 9 inches before the top and insert a 9-inch zipper by hand or machine.

Looking for the silver lining *is easy when you're wearing this peasant-style sweater. The color-through-color technique explained on page 30 was used to create the pattern. Design: Pamela Hinchcliffe.*

Creative Crochet
to tempt & inspire you

This chapter features photographs of work done by advanced crocheters. Sometimes whimsical, sometimes serious, these creations are meant to intrigue and inspire you.

To complement these photos are instructions for some advanced stitches and techniques that you may wish to try after mastering the basics of crochet.

All pieces shown here have been made by artists who have selected crochet as their medium of expression. By studying the unusual relationships of shapes and the unique color choices they have used, you can tell that some of these artists are also painters or sculptors. None of the pieces was made from a pattern; all of them "grew" as they were made. This "growing" process is intrinsic to crochet as to no other medium since the work goes so very quickly when in experienced hands.

Cossack costume? *(Etruscan, Tartar, Mongolian?) No, it's simply a crocheted wool caftan—a guaranteed party stopper. Design: Bonnie Britton.*

Jumbo sculpture, *3 feet high, was crocheted, woven, and stuffed. You can use it as a corner brightener or for a playroom punching bag. Design: Bonnie Britton.*

Show Stoppers

Grandmother's button box *produced the decorative materials for this unusual necklace of soft, muted tones. First the backing was crocheted and then the buttons were sewn on with matching yarn. Design: Bonnie Britton.*

Advanced Stitches

Some advanced stitches call for inserting the crochet hook in a different-from-usual manner to create a textural change in the pattern.

Working under One Loop

Working in the back of a stitch produces a ribbed effect (see afghan on the cover and on page 60). Instead of putting the hook under both strands of yarn into the top of the stitch, you insert the hook under the back strand only. At the end of the row, turn and continue in the same manner. (The rows of stitches will look as if they are lying on top of each other.)

To pick up the other side of a chain, turn your work upside down, with the bottom of the foundation chain facing you. Take a new strand of yarn and insert hook under only loop left on chain. (You went under the two top loops when you made your first row of stitches.) Continue working stitch in normal manner across row of chains, inserting hook under one loop of chain for each stitch.

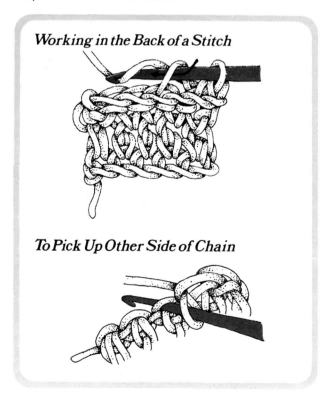

Working in the Back of a Stitch

To Pick Up Other Side of Chain

Crocheting between Stitches

A technique most commonly used in making granny squares (see vests, page 37), the "space" refers to the chains that have been worked between the double crochets. The space, then, is the opening left below the chains. **To crochet into a space,** insert the hook around the chains into the opening.

When there are no chains to make an opening, you work in the small spaces between the stitches in a row. **To work between the stitches,** insert the hook from front to back through the small openings between the stitches.

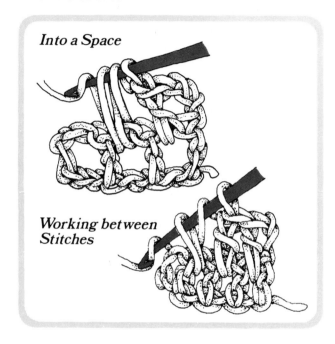

Into a Space

Working between Stitches

Working from Back to Front

A technique sometimes called for when working advanced stitches, working from back to front creates rows opposite from one another.

To work from back to front, insert the hook directly into the top of the stitch, from the back to the front.

Working from Back to Front

Working around the Post

Passing the hook behind the stitch adds dimension to the flat surface of your piece. To create this effect, make a row of double crochet, ch 3, turn. Yo, insert hook in between 1st and 2nd dc of previous row and out between the 2nd and 3rd dc **[A]**. Yo and complete stitch as in a normal dc **[B]** (see Basic Stitches, page 15).

Two advance stitches using the "working-around-the-post" technique are discussed below.

Working around the Post

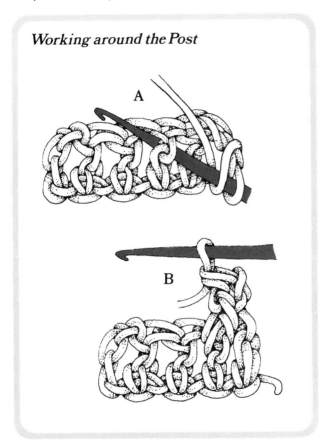

Cable-around-the-Post Stitch

To make the cable-around-the-post stitch, you work a regular double crochet, but you work it around the post. It always appears on the same side of the work.

Row 1: Work a row of dc, ch 3, turn.

Row 2: Yo, insert hook from the front in between the 1st and 2nd dc of the previous row and out again between the 2nd and 3rd dc. Yo and pull yarn through (3 lps on hook). Yo and pull yarn through 2 lps on hook (2 lps on hook). Yo and pull yarn through 2 lps on hook (1 lp on hook). Continue in this manner across row. Ch 3, turn.

Row 3: Work another row of dc as above, only insert the hook from the back of your work to the front, bring the hook in front of the stitch, and then bring it back out behind the stitch **[A]**.

Cable-around-the-Post Stitch

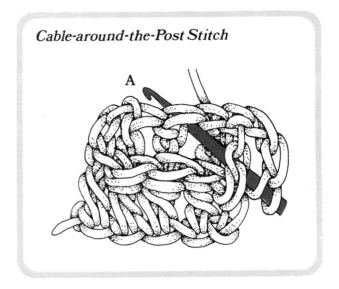

Shell-around-the-Post Stitch

Shell-around-the-post, like cable-around-the-post, is also based on double crochet.

Make a row of chs. Work 1 dc in 2nd ch from hook, 1 dc in next ch, yo **[A]**, insert hook in between the 1st and 2nd dc, yo, pull through, * yo, insert hook again, yo, pull through, rep from * 1x. Yo **[B]**, draw hook through all lps on hook. You have completed one shell-around-the-post **[C]**. Work 1 dc, then 1 shell around it to end of row.

Shell-around-the-Post Stitch

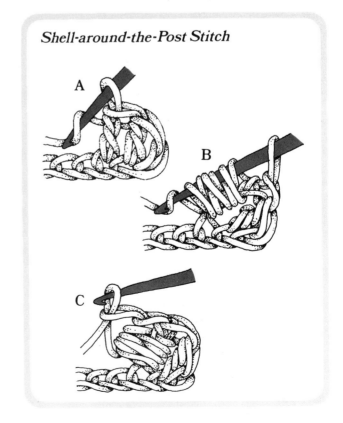

"Grandma! What big eyes you have!"
Actually, this is a friendly canine, crocheted
of yarn spun from the sheared fur of a
generous poodle. Design: Mary Moser.

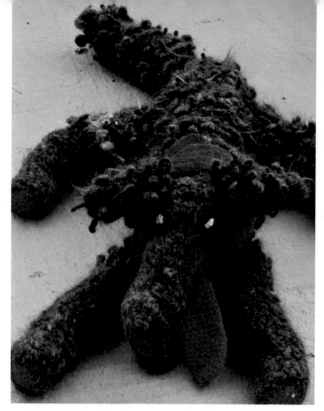

Monster hat, complete with horns, can turn
mild-mannered child into terror of the
neighborhood. Design: Lynne Morrall.

Whimsy

Hand spun alpaca,
traditional wool, and
linen were combined
in "Hooded Thistle
Cape for the Forest."
Design: Lori Hanson.

"Headdress for the Summer Sun of Peru" was
created from spotted feathers, waxed linen, wool,
and jute. Design: Lori Hanson.

Advanced Stitches

Popcorn Stitch

Used to make the bumps on the belt shown on pages 48-49, the popcorn stitch creates a bumpy effect true to its name.

1) Make several rows of single or double crochet or a row of chains.
2) Dc in 3rd st (or ch) from hook, ch 1, 5 dc in next ch, remove hook from lp, insert hook into 1st of the 5 dc, pick up dropped lp **[A]** and pull it through, ch 1 (one popcorn stitch made) **[B]**.
3) Continue across row, working 1 dc in next st (or ch), ch 1, 1 popcorn st, and so forth.

Popcorn Stitch

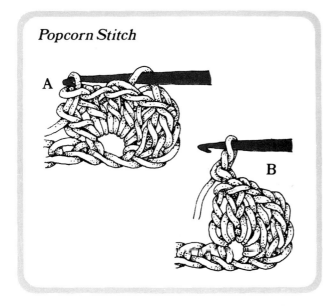

Cluster Stitch

The cluster stitch gathers several stitches into one puffy stitch.

Make several rows of single or double crochet or a row of chains.

Row 1: Yo and insert hook in 4th ch (or appropriate st) from hook, yo and draw through 1 lp, yo and draw through 2 lps, yo and insert hook in next ch (or st), yo and draw through 1 lp, yo **[A]** and draw through 2 lps, yo and draw through the 3 lps on hook **[B]**, * ch 2, sk 2 chs (or sts), (yo, insert hook into next ch, yo and draw through 1 lp, yo and draw through 2 lps)3x, yo and draw through the 4 lps on hook, ch 1. Rep from * across.

Row 2: * (Yo, insert hook in top lp of cl of previous row, draw through 1 lp, yo and draw through 2 lps)2x, yo and draw through 3 lps on hook, ch 2, rep from * across. Ch 1, turn.

Row 3: Rep row 2 for pattern.

Cluster Stitch

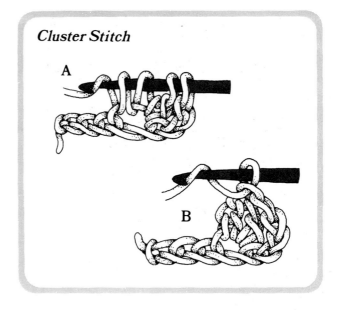

Double Chain

Sometimes referred to as a chain of single crochets, the double chain gives your work a sturdier base than a regular chain does. A double chain can also be used for a cord or tie or for trim.

1) Make a slip knot and 2 regular chs.
2) Insert hook into 2nd ch from hook and work 1 sc.
3) * Insert hook under left lp of sc you have just made. Yo **[A]** and draw through 1 lp (2 lps left on hook **[B]**. Yo and draw through both lps. Rep from * until ch is desired length.

Double Chain

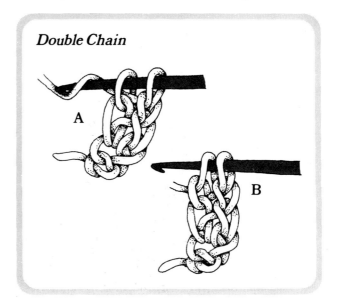

"Strawberry Vest" combines crochet and sewing techniques. Stuffed fabric accents were appliquéd to crocheted shell; cotton lining and sleeve cuffs add finishing touches. Design: Janet Lipkin.

"Ceramasnowethylene Queen Scene" is a body sculpture made of strips of clear plastic crocheted around glossy ceramic rings. Design: Lois Jane Hadfield.

Eye-catching vest is crocheted of hand spun, vegetable-dyed yarn. Strips of natural fleece down center of piece create furry front. Design: Mary Moser.

Baby's first blouse *grew from a basic granny square (see page 37). Mother used a ready-made shirt for a pattern. Design: Tonya Carpenter.*

A Rainbow of Finery

Coat of many colors *keeps its owner both warm and regally clothed. Design: Pamela Hinchcliffe.*

Peacock coat *displays an impressive range of perfectly compatible colors, stitch variations. Color-through-color technique (see page 30) was used throughout. Design: Pamela Hinchcliffe.*

Advanced Stitches

Double-Thick Double Crochet

Made entirely of double crochet, this double-faced technique creates an effect similar to that of double-knit fabric.

Make a ch of about 20 sts.

Row 1: Dc in each ch across, ch 3, turn.

Row 2: Sk 1st st, * yo, insert hook into back lp of 2nd dc of previous row and down into the back lp of 2nd ch. (Keep hook perpendicular to the row of sts.) Yo **[A]** and pull through both back lps, yo and pull through 2 lps on hook, yo and pull through last 2 lps on hook. Rep from * across row. Ch 3, turn **[B]**.

Row 3: Yo, insert hook in back lp of 2nd dc and in back lp of 2nd dc of previous row. Yo and complete a regular dc. Dc in each dc across row, working in the back lps as before. Ch 3, turn.

Loop Stitch

Unusual because it is formed on the back side of your work, the loop stitch can add a distinctive touch or form an unusual border. You can make the loops any size, but to keep the size consistent, use a piece of cardboard for a template. The loops can be left loopy or cut for a shaggy effect.

Make a row of chs.

Row 1: Make a row of sc. Ch 1, turn.

Row 2: * Wrap yarn around index finger from back to front (just the opposite of the way you would normally wrap the yarn). Insert hook into st, pass hook over and behind the strand that goes behind your finger, and catch the strand that goes in front of your finger **[A]**. Draw these 2 lps through (3 lps on hook). Drop the lp off your index finger, yo **[B]** and pull through all 3 lps on hook in one motion. You have completed 1 lp st **[C]**. Rep from * across row, working 1 lp st in each st. Ch 1, turn.

Row 3: Work a row of sc. Ch 1, turn.

Row 4: Rep row 2.

Continue, alternating between a row of sc and a row of lp st.

Double-Thick Double Crochet

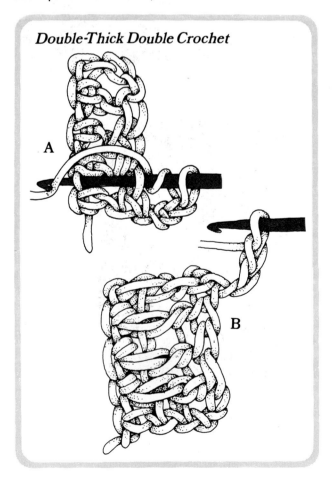

Loop Stitch

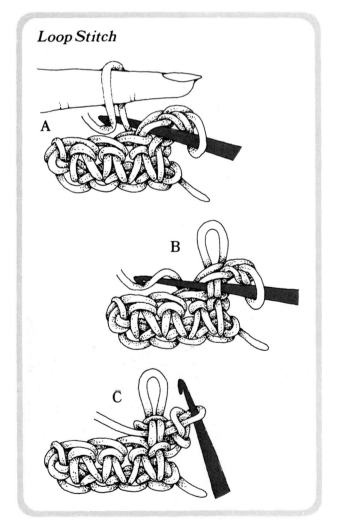

Avant-garde Accessories

Tiny fruits and vegetables *embellish combination wallet-purse. The edibles were crocheted separately, then appliquéd to the purse. Polychrome rainbow serves as wallet's fastener. Design: Toni Ach Lowenthal.*

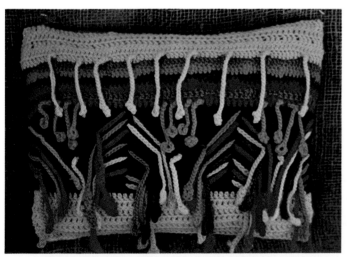

This little piggy *is a bank. Standing 8 inches tall, his crocheted body is made of soft wool; his ears are of mohair. Design: Judy Kleinberg.*

Miniature companions *for a table top: California Victorian home and a palm tree. Design: Mary Moser.*

Crocheted ginger jar *and basket can hold straw flowers, loose change, or potpourri. Design: Laurie Smith.*

"Pillow with Floppy Things" *is a smashing combination of brilliant colors and crocheted textural surface decoration. Design: Helen Bitar.*

Index

Photographers

Karel Bauer: 74 (bottom left, bottom right). **Richard Bermack:** 32. **Glenn M. Christiansen:** back cover (all), 33, 34 (all), 36, 37, 39, 42 (all), 44, 45, 47 (all), 49 (all), 51, 54, 56 (all), 59, 62 (all), 66, 68, 69, 70, 71 (all), 74 (top left, top right), 76 (bottom right), 77 (top left), 79 (top left, top right, bottom right). **Arthur Decker:** 76 (top). **Adrienne Digiesi:** 77 (bottom left, middle right). **Lois Jane Hadfield:** 76 (bottom left). **Judith I. Kleinberg:** 79 (middle). **Norman A. Plate:** 57, 64. **Eric Silverstein:** 79 (bottom left). **Darrow M. Watt:** 4, 6, 9 (all), 10, 13, 14, 15, 16, 17, 18 (all), 21, 22, 23, 24, 25, 26 (all), 28, 29.